THE ORVIS® GUIDE TO

SMALL STREAM FLY FISHING

THE
ORVIS®
GUIDE TO
SMALL STREAM FLY FISHING

———— ✠ ————

TOM ROSENBAUER

UNIVERSE

Published by Universe Publishing

A Division of Rizzoli International Publications, Inc.

300 Park Avenue South

New York, NY 10010

www.rizzoliusa.com

Project Editor: Candice Fehrman
Book Design: Lori S. Malkin
Text and Photography: Tom Rosenbauer

2011 2012 2013 2014 / 10 9 8 7 6 5 4 3 2 1

Printed in China

ISBN-13: 978-0-7893-2225-8

Library of Congress Catalog Control Number: 2010935638

Dedicated to Brooke, Brett, and Robin.

The loves of my life.

———⫸⫷———

Table of Contents

 **Foreword** ....

When Tom Rosenbauer asked me to write a foreword for his new small-stream book, I had mixed feelings. Tom and I have been friends a long time; we've fished together on small streams and big rivers spread across a couple of continents. And I was raised to believe that when a friend asks for a favor, you don't hesitate to act.

Plus, even before I read the manuscript I knew it would be a worthwhile book, because Tom isn't just a dyed-in-the-hare's-ear small-stream fetishist; he's also the most relentlessly analytical fly fisherman I know. Maybe it's that university degree in fisheries biology. Maybe it's a genetically questing nature. Maybe it's that wide-eyed youthful hunger for knowledge that most of us had as children but which in Tom still burns, unextinguished by time.

I remember years ago fishing in Colorado and hearing all this whooping and hollering and manic laughter echoing through a vast mountain stillness—kind of like entering a cathedral to find a 12-year-old on the back bench enthralled by a new video game he couldn't quite master. I rounded a bend and looked downstream, and there was Rosenbauer, kneeling on the far bank and poking his rod from behind the sagebrush, dapping an invisible fly on the water and getting splashy refusals. Every time the fish spurned his fly, Tom tried a different angle, or a different cast, or a different drift, and eventually a different fly, each time learning something new. Finally a confident geyser erupted, and Tom's rod bent double and then almost instantly went slack: the big brown he'd been pestering the past hour had finally taken his fly, and then just as quickly broke him off. The kind of person I prefer not to fish with would have slashed the water with his rod and stomped his feet and yelled a lot of very bad words. But Tom just laughed even harder, tied on a new fly, and then inched on upstream, looking for more entertainment, more opportunities to learn something new.

And so, speaking in my several roles as Tom's friend, as a lunatic-fringe small-stream trout fisherman for the past half century, as a writer and editor of books and magazines about fishing and the outdoors for the past quarter century, I can say without hesitation that I know of no one better qualified to write the essential primer on fly fishing small streams than Tom Rosenbauer. I learned something on every page of this book—just as I learned something around every bend when we fished a brace of small secret streams near his home in Vermont. These beautiful pages, so dense with information yet so effortless to read, are a testament to the careful craftsmanship you'd expect from a small-stream specialist and a thoughtful writer. My publishing antennae think this book could easily go beyond being yet another fly-fishing how-to and become the inspiration for a whole new generation of small-stream trout fishers, drawn to these undersized realms for all the right reasons.

And yet . . .

And yet for purely selfish reasons I'm not all that sure I want my favorite places on this planet clotted up with hordes of new anglers. For me, the attraction of small trout streams is their lonely untrammeled peace. In a world increasingly crowded, they are tiny islands of solace that, with the proper approach and the proper attitude, can offer immense rewards to those in search of small contentments.

But maybe I shouldn't worry. Fly fishers these days seem mostly inspired by magazine covers featuring buff dudes wearing flashy clothes and brandishing big fish caught from name-brand waters, where their long, carefully schooled casts unfurl like

James Babb fishes a small stream in East Tennessee's Cherokee National Forest.

candy canes beneath the big sky. But on a small stream, there's no room for that beautiful school-room cast. Trees lean in from all sides; a tunnel of entangling mountain laurel awaits your flawless backcast and snazzy duds. The soft spot by that rock where a trout would lie is barely two rod-lengths away, and your bushy dry fly has to land in a spot the size of a dinner plate with enough slack in the leader so it doesn't instantly drag. You get one chance, with no backcast, with no margin for error. You're not standing brave against the sky; you're probably balanced on one knee and clinging to a root with one hand. And your reward, if you make the cast and don't fall *splat* into the pool? A wild trout the length of a dollar bill, most likely. A really big one might stretch to two dollar bills and a fifty-cent piece. Try *that* for a magazine cover.

And yet you'll learn more about fly fishing messing around with those dinky trout on those nameless little streams than in any of those schools, on any of those big famous rivers. And if you're the kind of person I hope you are, you'll enjoy it more, too.

I could type myself to a nub trying to explain what's so captivating about fishing small trout streams. Or I could just steal the best thing I ever read on the subject, from the 19th-century Maine writer Sarah Orne Jewett, who wrote this in her classic, *The Country of the Pointed Firs*:

"If there is one way above another of getting so close to nature that one simply is a piece of nature, following a primeval instinct with perfect self-forgetfulness and forgetting everything except the dreamy consciousness of pleasant freedom, it is to take the course of a shady trout brook. The dark pools and the sunny shallows beckon one on; the wedge of sky between the trees on either bank, the speaking, companioning noise of the water, the amazing importance of what one is doing, and the constant sense of life and beauty make a strange transformation of the quick hours."

Small trout streams are where I've spent some of the best moments of my life. That so few people visit them today seems in the short term a blessing for us solitary old coots. But given how often wild places without vocal constituencies find themselves industrially violated these days, that seems a very shortsighted and selfish view.

So maybe I should look on the readers of this book not as future competition, but as a new generation of like-minded souls drawn to visit, and love, and therefore protect the kinds of anonymous small places that nourish our roots—as anglers, as naturalists, as conservationists, as human beings.

JAMES R. BABB, Editor,
Gray's Sporting Journal

Introduction

I have enjoyed a lifelong love affair with small trout streams. It began with a paper route in suburban Rochester, New York. I had been fishing since I was out of diapers, and although my father, who instilled my love of fishing, was a bait fisherman, I soon became interested in fly fishing instead. I almost wore out the three fly-fishing books in my local library by the time I was 12. My early fly fishing was restricted to places I could reach on my bike, mostly for tiny bass in a pond behind the high school and for white perch and sunfish in the bays off Lake Ontario.

My favorite spot on my paper route was the home of Art Pierce, an old crippled man who lived in a wheelchair, but had once been a serious walleye and lake trout fisherman. Collection day was the high point of the week; after counting out his quarters for the weekly news, Mr. Pierce would regale me of glory days on Seneca Lake trolling for giant lakers. My routine was to always ask him, "Were they biting?" I knew he would suddenly rise out of his chair and exclaim, "Were they bitin'? Jeezus Keerist was they bitin'!" His wife would roll her eyes while my good Catholic upbringing took delight in hearing a grown man swear while talking to me and not another adult. One day the subject settled on brook trout and I told Mr. Pierce that I really wanted to catch one, but had never even seen one.

"Well Jeezus, you got speckled trout in that little stream right off Huntington Lane. That's on your paper route, right?" Of course I took the remark as more of his raving about bygone days and didn't really even want to hope I had brook trout within a half mile of my house. But I couldn't get the idea out of my head, so one October Friday my best fishing buddy Leigh and I took our rods into the dense woods north of Huntington Lane, where a large tract of undeveloped land ran up against a golf course before hitting the shores of Lake Ontario. We caught a few creek chubs in the lower stretches of the creek before working upstream into its spring-fed headwaters. The stream opened into a shaded glade where the water ran over clean gravel. Suddenly we saw fish. It seemed like hundreds of them in shallow water, darting into deeper water when we got close, and they didn't have the same dull brown color and slow movements of the creek chubs we were used to. These fish were a speckled dark green and blue, with fins edged in sharp black-and-white lines and bellies so bright orange they looked on fire. There had been wild brook trout under my nose all those years I'd been riding my bike to catch sunfish and white perch.

I'd like to tell you we caught those fish on dry flies and released them. We didn't. We wormed them and netted them so we could admire their colors, and we took them home for dinner. In subsequent years we learned how to swing a Parmachene Belle wet fly through the riffles and fish a Yellow Humpy dry fly along the undercut banks in the evening when the fish were rising. But to a 12-year-old, the sign of a successful angler was bringing the fish home for Mom and Dad to enjoy, fried in butter or bacon grease for breakfast.

On Saturday morning I rode my bike as fast as I could pedal to Mr. Pierce's house so I could share our discovery with him. There were cars parked in his driveway and all along the street near his house, so I kept on riding and planned on telling him about it the next collection day. But on Sunday in Mass we were asked to pray for the soul of Art Pierce, among a few other people, and it was one of the greatest regrets of my young life that I never got to hear him exclaim, "Jeezus Keerist, I told you they were there!"

This began my lifelong love affair with small streams. Although blasting a streamer into a school of bluefin tuna crashing on the surface or presenting a tiny dry fly to a 20-inch brown trout on a calm pool in a giant river both get my blood pumping, there is something about small streams—perhaps something hard-wired into my brain at that impressionable age—that commands me to imagine what kind of trout are in every tiny rivulet I drive by on the highway. I'm hardly alone in this passion for tiny waters and (mostly) tiny fish. I talk with people all over the country who also profess a love for small-stream trout fishing. Perhaps most of them started with an adolescent impression as well.

The other day Bill Reed, a friend and colleague and fellow small-stream addict, walked into my office and whispered, "I heard Rick has been crushing the browns in XYZ Creek." Translation: Our friend Rick, another small-stream junkie, was having great luck catching brown trout in XYZ Creek. I've substituted "XYZ" for the real name of the creek, because small-stream anglers are very secretive about their favorite spots. These tiny gems are not like most trout streams today, where you can pull up a fishing report on the Internet less than 24 hours old that gives information on everything from hatches to water temperatures to GPS coordinates for the best access points. Most tiny streams stay secret, like in the old days before the Internet, when to get information about a trout stream you had to spend a lot of time in bars, keeping your ears open for slips of the tongue by guys with wrinkles in their pant legs from hours of wearing waders and the telltale smell of insect repellent.

Bill was whispering because only a few weeks earlier another colleague, Brett, had moved to a new town that has a cute little rocky stream running right through the center (which consists of a general store and a few houses). I made the mistake of asking Brett if he'd ever fished that little stream and he answered that he hadn't and it looked a little shallow to be a decent trout stream. I mentioned that he might want to try it and a few days later he came into the office with a wild look in his eyes. "I can't believe how many trout are in that stream!" he said. "I caught about 15 nice browns and brook trout, all on dry flies." Not really tuned into the small-stream code, Brett told a few friends who told a few other friends, and now instead of remaining a forgotten stream that Bill and I could fish whenever we wanted to without running into anyone, we might expect to find several cars parked in the few pull-offs along the Brook Road.

People who enjoy small-stream trout fishing with a fly have different values than other anglers. Or at least they do when they are in small-stream mode. Bill and I are passionate about fishing for big, selective trout on large, famous rivers; we lose sleep on nights before taking a trip to the tropics to fish for bonefish or tarpon. We dream about chasing bluefin tuna 20 miles offshore with a 12-weight rod, yet we also delight in catching seven-inch brook trout that hardly put a bend in a fly rod and are as easy to fool as a kitten is with a piece of yarn. To us, it's not always about an epic battle with a fish that might break your tippet or a chess match trying to determine what a wise old fish is eating or the anticipation of hooking an Atlantic salmon after thousands of casts. Sometimes it's just nice to catch lots of easy fish with no other anglers or boats shattering the solitude.

Small-stream angling is also about the discovery, the journey, the unknown. I like nothing better than to begin fishing a small stream I've never tried before, working upstream at a pace of my choosing, with the whole day in front of me. And once I've discovered a good one, I like to revel in my secret, keeping the stream in my back pocket, knowing that the next time I need a break from office politics, worrying about the value of my 401(k), or even dealing with snotty trout on heavily fished streams, I'll have a place to get back to the essence of fly fishing, with a single box of flies, a floating line, and a short, lightweight rod. And easy fish to boost my ego.

It may take me a long time to run out of new places to uncover. I've lived in southern Vermont for 33 years and still drive by little trout streams on my 35-minute commute to work that I've never fished, plus miles of water on other streams that I have fished, just not those particular stretches. Some of them I can jump across (my legs aren't very long) and may only serve up six-inch trout—but the wonder of discovery won't be lost, because you never know what a small stream will offer until you try it. When I drive to other states or fly over them, I'm always looking at little ribbons of clear water, wondering if they hold trout, what species of trout, how big the trout might be, and if anyone ever bothers to fish the streams with a fly rod. Tiny New Jersey, the most densely populated state in the United States, has 59 small wild brook trout streams that have been discovered by researchers with Trout Unlimited's Eastern Brook Trout Joint Venture, and probably countless more that support wild brown trout and hatchery browns and rainbows. That's enough small-stream fishing for a lifetime—in *New Jersey*.

I haven't fished any small streams in New Jersey, but I'd like to someday. I haven't chased small-stream trout in many other states, but I have spent the better part of 45 years exploring miniature trout waters every place I could, and have talked to other small-stream addicts in the places I haven't seen. In this book, I hope to give you a new understanding of what makes small streams tick, how you can discover your own small streams, and, of course, the techniques you can use to pluck magnificent little creatures, most of them as wild as trout in any wilderness area, from streams in your backyard or at least within a short drive of your home or vacation spot.

What's a Small Stream?

 **Chapter 1** ....

What's a Small Stream and Why Should You Be Interested?

Small Streams Defined

For the purposes of this book, a small trout stream is any stream where an angler would not spend more than 10 minutes in a single pool. It's a stream where a single cast will reach from one end of the pool to another. It's a stream that won't appear in a feature article in a magazine. A stream where you'll see few people and even fewer anglers— you may see more photographers and skinny-dippers than people wearing waders. And, OK, if you have to pin me down, it will typically be less than 30 feet wide. But be careful of that width parameter, because Nelson's Spring Creek in the Paradise Valley of

PAGES 22–23: Small-stream anglers have most streams to themselves, and don't have to worry about boat traffic.

OPPOSITE: Although Nelson's Spring Creek is small water, it is rich with insect life and heavily fished. It is better fished with standard trout techniques used for selective trout, not the specialized small-stream techniques in this book.

Montana is less than 30 feet wide, and it's been written up in countless magazines back as far as Joe Brooks's *Outdoor Life* columns in the 1960s; it often has as many anglers on it as the landowners, the Nelson family, will allow; and an angler could happily spend four hours in one pool because there are so many trout in this productive little spring creek that one seldom gets the itch to wander.

But here we are talking about the small trout streams most people ignore, not the ones they are drawn to. These are trout streams that are disregarded by most anglers because they seldom produce big fish. But there are good, serious anglers who get wildly excited about tiny wild trout in wild environments. I once flew hundreds of miles and then drove three hours to fish for brook trout in the Smoky Mountains with Scott Farfone. Scott is a guide and fly shop owner who has fished from Montana to the Bahamas and has done it all his life. He and his guides fish the South Holston, one of the best trout rivers in the country and home to giant brown trout. Yet Scott and I spent our time in creeks along the Blue Ridge Parkway that hold less water than a respectable drainage ditch, and we both got wildly excited when Scott threw a small streamer into a plunge pool the size of a hot tub and the biggest trout he had ever seen on that creek made a pass at his fly. After catching his breath Scott blurted, "My god, that fish must have been eleven inches long!"

Why Bother with Small Streams and Their Dinky Trout?

If you have never fished for small-stream trout, it will probably take some convincing before you try it. Fish from small streams look insignificant in still pictures or on video. Even from a nearby road or walking path, they don't look like anything you'd want to fish. My English friend Barry Unwin and I were driving through Rocky Mountain National Park one fall, in search of a trout stream highly recommended by a local fly fisher. Barry and I both love small-stream fishing for the solitude and pure trout fishing experience it provides, but from the road we both thought the stream looked a little thin and not worth exploring. We finally decided to try the stream, and by the time we had scampered down the bank and stepped into the water, we were immersed in its world with complete abandon. The pools were deeper than they looked from the road, the riffles were far more complex than they appeared from 50 feet above, and we soon found ourselves challenged by the eight-inch browns and rainbows as much as if we'd been fishing a world-famous stream filled with 20-inch brown trout.

Although trout in small streams are tiny compared to the trout most of us expect to catch, when

Scott Farfone gets excited about small wild trout in an intimate setting.

If you plan to enjoy small-stream fishing, you have to get as excited over a small brook trout as my friend John D'Arbeloff.

the Pacific drainage. But typically even the invasive species will be what anglers call "wild" fish, which means they've never seen the inside of a fish hatchery and their fins are clean and sharp-edged.

Small streams are too shallow and narrow for drift boats or inner tubes, so they can be enjoyed in solitude. Even other anglers are rare, and many small streams, even in popular trout destinations, may see only a few different fly fishers a year. Most anglers scoff at the small trout, don't even know the trout exist, or worry about catching their fly in streamside brush. The few fly fishers that take the time to explore a small stream will give a wide berth to others. I won't fish within a mile of another person on a small stream knowing that I can walk way ahead of him or her, or drive to another stream a few miles away. From what I've seen, most other small-stream anglers have the same philosophy.

This is fly fishing that brings you back to its essence. One rod with a floating line will do it. More than one box of flies is overkill. You will seldom have to carry more than two spools of tippet material, a net is useless baggage, strike indicators just fill up the space in your pocket that could be more usefully occupied by a granola bar, and you don't have to worry about that stained shirt because no one will see you. It's pure stalking, casting, and catching. Your leader won't be weighted down with split shot and bobbers. It's an intimate world, where your face might be inches away from a trout as you creep around the side of a boulder to make a stunted cast in the plunge pool above you.

Fish in small streams are not always pushovers, but they'll be easier to catch than the fish in most large rivers. They're easier to locate. The shallow nature of small streams restricts fish to narrow lanes and pockets that form the deepest parts of the streambed. In larger rivers, as much as three-quarters of the water you see may be devoid of trout more than six inches long, but in small streams, trout populations are denser as long as there is decent habitat to support them, so every little slot may hold fish.

you put it in relative terms, where else can you go where every fish you hook swims from one side of the pool to the other, and might run from the tail of the pool to the head during the battle? Still, these fish seldom put much of a bend in your rod and they hardly ever pull line from your reel—backing is as useful as bear spray in a Nebraska cornfield. Sometimes the fish are so small that if you set the hook with too much enthusiasm they go flying through the air and back over your shoulder.

Small-stream fish are gorgeous. Most often bred in the stream you are fishing, they are sleek and colorful. They are true wild creatures, and if you are very fortunate they will be indigenous to the stream you're fishing, like brook trout in the Appalachians, cutthroats in the Rockies, or rainbows on the western slope of the Sierras. They might be invasive species, too, like brown trout anywhere in the world except Europe or Asia, or rainbow trout outside of

And trout in small streams are more likely to see your fly, because as much as we like to think we are scratching bottom with a weighted nymph or streamer in larger rivers, the fact is the current conspires to pull our flies toward the surface with most presentations deeper than a few feet, and there is invariably some deep, fast water that you just cannot get a fly down to, or, if you can, a natural, drag-free drift lasts only a few inches before the flow tugs on your line and leader and moves the fly out of the strike zone. In small streams, a dry fly can be seen by most fish, and it's no sweat to get a nymph to drift just above the bottom for the entire pool when the pool is only 10 feet long and two feet deep.

The Small-Stream Environment

Many of the small streams you'll fish are considered first-order or second-order streams in a hierarchical system called the Strahler Order by hydrologists. A first-order stream is a perennial stream that is unforked; in other words its water is mostly from a single source, either a spring, or series of springs, or snow or rain runoff that finally coalesces into a permanent streambed that stays wetted year-round. When two first-order streams join, they form a second-order stream. Only two second-order streams can form a third-order stream; if a first-order stream joins a second-order stream it remains a second-order stream. The point is that most of these small streams get their water from a restricted source that is uniform in characteristics until these streams flow lower into a valley and get warmer and slower.

The water in first-order streams is unlike the flow in larger rivers in more ways than just volume. The water is close to its source, and the source is most likely either groundwater or snow melt. (Even though the water coming into first-order streams may be dependent on rainfall, it is usually rainfall that has seeped through the ground and then re-emerged as springs. Streams entirely dependent on surface rainfall will dry up when there is no rain, so they'll hold little

aquatic life.) Small streams stay colder during the summer. If they're fed by groundwater as springs, water comes out of the ground at about the annual mean temperature of a given latitude, which in the far northern United States is about 42 degrees and in the mountains of western North Carolina is about 62 degrees. In most of the mountain areas of the western United States, where you find most small streams, it ranges from 45 to 55 degrees. The important point is that small streams will stay well within the comfort level for trout even in the hottest weather, and when larger rivers lower in a valley are pushing the lethal limits for trout, above 72 degrees, small streams, closer to the source, will be well within the limit for active, healthy trout feeding.

Streams fed mostly by groundwater are also healthier in the winter. Because the water is warmer than the air, these streams are less likely to form anchor ice, when water freezes from the bottom of the stream up and, if thick enough, can snuff out aquatic life. Bigger rivers, unless they are "tailwater" rivers (rivers with a controlled flow below dams), will reflect the air temperature instead of groundwater temperature and will often be colder and less productive for fishing during the winter and early spring. Streams fed by snow or glacier melt don't offer the protection of warmer winter flows, but they do stay cold during the heat of the summer.

First-order streams are also low in nutrients and dissolved oxygen, which limits their food supply. Most trout streams derive their productivity from single-celled algae, diatoms, bacteria, and fungi that form a "biofilm," which coats rocks and woody debris in the streambed. Just as important is woody debris that falls into the stream as it courses through woodlands and meadows, which provides nutrients for these microorganisms. Aquatic insects feed on both this biofilm and on the dead leaves and wood that flow with the current. Close to the source of groundwater, microorganisms have not had a chance to gain a foothold (as anyone who drinks well water is aware), and little terrestrial vegetation has fallen into the water. So the farther down the course of a stream you go, the richer it gets, because it has had a chance to accumulate more detritus and algae, providing food for the aquatic insects and crustaceans that trout eat. Sunlight helps as well, because algae need sunlight to survive. Knowing this, you can now predict that a rocky stream flowing through dense woods, but without a lot of logs and branches in the water, will have a sparse food supply. Hatches will be very few and trout will be tiny. A rocky stream high in the Sierras of California might not offer much woody debris, but its wide-open streambed lets the sun in and encourages algae growth. So fish here might be bigger, even though the environment looks pretty sterile. Rocky streams with stretches of woodland or meadow that get both adequate sunlight and terrestrial vegetation will offer decent hatches of aquatic insects and bigger fish.

A special kind of first-order stream is one that emerges from the ground through limestone bedrock, commonly known by fly fishers as a "spring creek." Limestone adds nutrients that encourage the growth of aquatic weeds, often very close to the source of the spring, and these streams, because they emerge from a valley floor, have a lower gradient. Instead of a rocky streambed, the bottom is silt, which helps rooted aquatic plants take hold. ("Limestone streams" are waters with the same rich water chemistry, but often have rocky bottoms. You can identify them because they have a slight gray milky tint to the water, even when the water is low, and you'll find aquatic weeds in slower water and a rich film of algae on most rocks.) Aquatic insects have a good source of food very close to the source of the stream, and additionally the high calcium content of the limestone groundwater enables aquatic crustaceans like scuds ("freshwater shrimp"), sow bugs ("pill bugs"), and crayfish to thrive.

I won't spend much time discussing spring creeks or limestone streams in this book. They are so rich that they quickly take on the character of much larger rivers, and most of them are well-known and get a lot of fishing pressure. Thus, fishing in most spring creeks is more like fishing much larger rivers, with their correspondingly blasé, selective fish with an attitude, used to legions of anglers. The Letort and Spring Creek in Pennsylvania, the spring creeks of the Paradise Valley in Montana, and Hot Creek in California are typical examples. Although tiny in flow, these streams see thousands of fly fishers a year. Let's stick to the easy fish and secluded waters of what anglers call "freestone" streams—in other words any stream that is not a spring creek or a tailwater. It's not like we're missing anything. For every spring creek or tailwater in North America, there are hundreds of small freestone streams that have never been betrayed on a Web site and might not see more than a half dozen fly fishers all season.

Small streams do a poor job of serving up a menu of aquatic insects because they lack the large expanses of riffles found in larger streams and rivers. Riffles offer the rocky substrate that aquatic insects need to protect themselves from the ravages of the current. They expose more air to carbon dioxide and oxygen, which are needed by aquatic algae to grow. Pools, in contrast, are virtual deserts. Although we know that trout live in riffles if the riffles offer deeper pockets and aquatic insects do live in pools, it's an oversimplification (but not that much of a stretch) to say that riffles produce the food and pools provide the slower current that makes it easier for trout to feed.

Now let's compare a trout in a pool in a large river to one in a tiny plunge pool in a small stream. Imagine both lay in the same current velocity, so it takes the same amount of effort for both of them to hold in the flow and pluck insects from the current. Given that most trout won't move more than a foot or two to either side to feed, the trout in the small stream has a riffle upstream of its position that might be 20 feet long at best. In contrast, the trout in a larger river could have more than 100 yards of food-producing riffle ahead of it. The trout in the larger river could have a food supply in the magnitude of 15 times that of the trout in the small stream. No wonder trout in small streams don't reach trophy proportions!

We've seen that these small freestone streams offer a sparse menu of aquatic insects. In fact, in many of them, it's doubtful that trout bigger than a few inches could grow, because the amount of food they get is not even enough to balance the daily activities of holding in the current and swimming away from predators. Luckily, terrestrial insects make up for the paucity of aquatic food. In fact, in many small streams ants, beetles, grasshoppers, flies, bees, wasps, caterpillars, and moths make up as much as 80 percent of the food supply.

Knowing this can benefit both your fly selection and your fly presentation. It also, in theory, makes small-stream trout less fussy about what fly pattern you use. Small-stream trout almost never see a dense hatch of one species of aquatic insects. And if they're feeding on a beetle one minute, a cricket the next, a tiny ant five minutes later, with a few moths mixed in, they are not going to develop a search image for a particular size or shape and stick with that type of food. They'll be drawn to those bugs they know are safe, but they will still grab anything that looks remotely edible because they never know when their next meal could drift by.

Judging the Relative Food Supply of a Small Stream

Food supply in small streams runs the gamut from sparse to very rich, and the size of trout you'll find corresponds to the food supply. Streams with abundant riparian vegetation will harbor more food than those that flow through rocky canyons, all other things being equal. Streams that are fed mainly by spring runoff, with frequent floods and an unstable

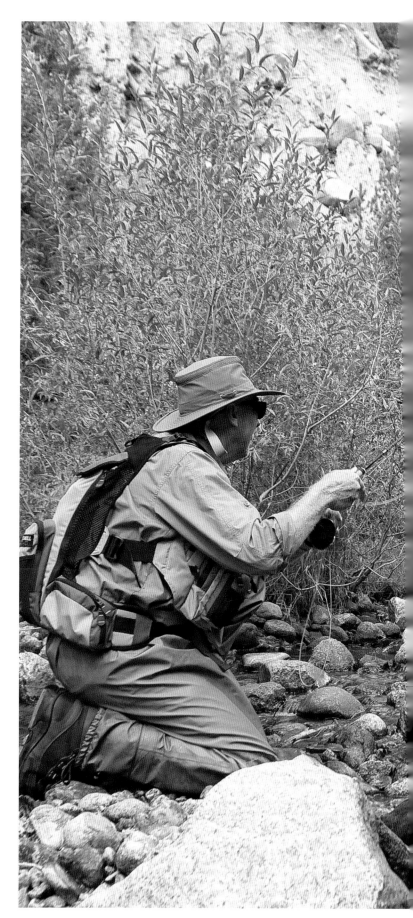

This is a first-order freestone stream high in the Colorado Rockies. The aquatic food supply is sparse and fish get much of their diet from terrestrial insects falling into the water.

streamside vegetation found mostly 10 feet or more from the banks? Are there dry, exposed gravel bars at every bend in the stream? All of these signs tell you the stream suffers frequent near-catastrophic floods that grind rocks and gravel along the bottom, making it a tough place for trout and aquatic insects to survive. Contrast this to streams where trees and shrubs grow right to the shore, indicating that flows in these streams are more stable.

Water chemistry also determines the amount of food in a small stream (whether it's a pocket-water stream or any of the others described). Water that flows over impermeable rocks like granite, quartzite, sandstone, and basalt picks up few nutrients, in particular calcium and magnesium salts, which seem to have a beneficial effect on aquatic plants and insects, as well as raising the pH, which reduces the acidity of water. Rainwater is naturally acidic, and in certain parts

flood plain, are not hospitable to aquatic insects so trout will be fewer and smaller. More stable pocket-water streams, fed mostly by springs, will produce more trout food per square foot and trout here will be larger and more numerous.

It's easy to determine the health of a stream by spending a few minutes studying its banks. Are there sticks and logs well above the existing waterline? Is

of the continent, especially on the East Coast, this natural acidity is increased because of air pollution. Limestone and marble bedrock are rich in nutrients and acid-neutralizing chemicals, and thus streams that run through belts of limestone will have a richer food supply, more trout, and bigger trout. You don't have to become a geologist to determine this, though, because these impermeable rocks are usually rounded and limestone occurs in flat sheets. Slate and shale, other flat rocks found on the beds of trout streams, are not as beneficial as limestone, but these rocks must offer some nutrients because I've found that streams with slate or shale bottoms are richer than streams that run through granite bedrock.

Water color can also give you a clue to the richness of a stream. Acidic streams often run through stands of conifers and bogs, and tannic acid leaching into the water gives it a brownish, tea-stained look. Small streams running through beds of limestone can take on a greenish, milky color, even during an extended drought. (Be careful in glacier country, though, because glaciers can also impart a milky color to streams and glacial water is notoriously nutrient-poor.) Crystal-clear water can be very infertile or quite fertile, though, depending on other factors, so if the water is clear you'll have to look for other hints.

Finally, aquatic vegetation, both larger aquatic plants and the biofilm on the rocks, indicate richer water. Rooted aquatic plants are easy to spot, but the presence of algae, diatoms, and fungi on rocks is just a little harder to determine. If rocks are slippery and seem to have a light film on them you can assume that the stream is relatively rich in food. If rocks look pristine, as though they've just been pressure-washed, trout food is probably sparse.

Types of Small Streams and How to Identify Them

Throughout this book, when recommending flies and techniques, I'll refer to different types of small streams because your tactics should vary with each of them. Although these distinctions between the streams are my own, the terms I've used to describe them are pretty standard, so if you're reading another book or talking to other anglers you'll have common ways to discuss them. Of course nothing in nature is clear-cut, especially when we're lumping and splitting (even the taxonomists can't agree on species of fish and bugs), and one little stream, in the course of a few miles, might exhibit characteristics of two or even three types of small streams. So don't try to pigeonhole every stream you fish into one of these tidy categories. Instead, simply get an idea of where it falls in the spectrum. It is important, though, to get some idea of what kind of stream you're about to explore, as the nature of a small stream can determine what flies to use, how you should approach the stream, and how dense the fish population will be.

■ HIGH-MOUNTAIN, STEEP-GRADIENT STREAMS

Trout have adapted to the highest mountain streams in North America, as long as they hold water throughout the year and stay ice-free at some part of the season. I don't know of any streams in the eastern United States that would fit my classification of a high-mountain stream, so you'll find these only in the rugged mountain ranges of the western United States and Canada. They are characterized by sparse streamside vegetation (or none at all), rocky bottoms, and deeper plunge pools separated by rushing cascades.

Don't be dissuaded by waterfalls high enough to block the upstream progress of fish in these streams. Populations of trout can exist in small reaches of water, and even though a trout may not be able to jump a high waterfall, there may be a population of fish above the waterfall that sustains itself, or there may be an alpine lake above the falls that constantly replenishes the water running out of it. California's native golden trout, for example, thrive in streams between 8,000 and 12,000 feet above sea level, and a trout here may spend its entire life in a section of stream less than 40 feet long.

It's a tough life in these high-altitude streams. Food is sparse because the water stays cold year-round, and nutrients are low, so the biofilm on the rocks is thin. The sparsely vegetated banks offer little food for aquatic insects and a paucity of terrestrial

OPPOSITE: A steep-gradient stream with a series of plunge pools provides lots of trout habitat in a short run of water.

insects for trout. As a result, fish here will be small but very hungry. However, these little streams are never found in less than spectacular settings, and you'll seldom have to share the water with anyone.

The window of opportunity for an angler here is limited. Prior to spring runoff it's still full winter at these altitudes, and once temperatures warm in spring the full force of runoff makes these streams muddy and unfishable. It's only when runoff subsides and warm summer days arrive that water temperatures reach the point where trout feed actively; with the onset of fall, water temperatures once again drop below a comfortable level for trout. But catch a high-mountain stream from July through September and you'll have a banner day. These fish have a short growing season, they'll eat about anything that looks remotely edible, and they'll feed throughout the day, so all that's needed is to get a fly in front of one. Because these waters are transparent, though, high-mountain fish are vigilant and a wrong move sends them scurrying for cover.

◼ POCKET-WATER STREAMS

Pocket-water streams are those with a high gradient, but are not as severe as high-mountain streams, so instead of frequent cascades and plunge pools you are more likely to see a steady progression of white water, pockets around boulders, and short riffles. You'll find these streams anywhere water runs into a valley or narrow canyon off the lower slopes of

Pocket water offers few true pools but lots of nooks and crannies for trout.

Trout in woodland riffle-and-pool streams will be harder to approach because of the slower water in their pools.

mountains and hills, from Maine to Alaska. Vegetation along the shores of pocket-water streams can be dense woodland or rocky canyon.

Despite currents that look too turbulent to support trout, when you get close to a pocket-water stream and begin to dissect it, you'll find tiny pools below jumbles of boulders, where the current runs against a steep bank or when the stream curves. A trout can comfortably live its entire life in one of these tiny pockets, and where a pocket-water stream is not separated from a larger river by impassable falls, larger fish can move upstream to spawn or to seek colder water in high summer. Pocket-water pools can sometimes be frustrating to fish because almost every little slot looks fishy, and you can go crazy trying to fish it all. It helps to get some idea of how much food is in a pocket-water stream (and, as a result, how dense the fish population is) so that you can either shoot your fly into just the prime places and move quickly, or fish each stretch more thoroughly.

WOODLAND RIFFLE-AND-POOL STREAMS

Woodland riffle-and-pool streams are lower yet in gradient than pocket-water streams. As a result, these streams offer more defined pools separated by shallow riffles. These streams are surrounded by mature vegetation and trout will be found in pools more often than in riffles. Whereas trout in pocket water are more widely distributed, fish in woodland streams will be concentrated in pools.

Where your pace in a pocket-water stream might be steady, woodland streams require a different approach. You'll want to quickly pass up the riffles (unless they have pockets in them more than a foot deep) and concentrate on the pools, but that doesn't mean rushing into the pools like an impatient commuter stepping onto a train. The fish in these pools will be spookier than those in pocket water, so you'll need to approach each pool with caution.

LOWLAND, BOGGY STREAMS

Lowland, boggy streams are characterized by slow, uniform flows. Some of these can go for miles without producing a riffle. They are usually deeper than meadow streams and are often lined with dense tangles of alders and willow. Sometimes the only relief from their monotony is a beaver pond, where the stream channel widens and slows even more.

Lowland, boggy streams are tough to wade and the banks are sometimes impenetrable. They are often easier to fish from a canoe or other small watercraft.

You might think trout in boggy streams are difficult to approach given their slow current, but this is seldom the case. The deeper water gives trout a sense of security, and boggy streams are usually tea-stained so visibility is low. The most difficult aspect of fishing boggy streams is getting to the water. The thick, low brush along their banks turns a streamside ramble into a struggle that seems to clutch at fly lines, landing nets, and straps. They are frequently too deep to wade, and even if the water is not over your waist, the muck that lies below it might add a foot or two to the effective depth.

So fishing boggy streams on foot can be a matter of finding a convenient opening, or thrashing along until you find a convenient beaver dam for a perch. For this reason, fly fishers who spend a lot of time in these waters prefer a canoe, kayak, or pontoon boat, moving stealthily upstream or downstream, and anchoring up where the water looks good.

And did I mention the flies? Mosquitoes and black flies thrive in boggy streams.

MEADOW STREAMS

Meadow streams are those surrounded by low brush, pasture, or grassland. They are usually found where the slope of the land forms a broad valley. Some exhibit the same riffle-and-pool character of woodland streams, but often meadow streams, because of their very low gradient, will form a series of deeper interconnected runs or pockets, with a short riffle at the head followed by a long, thin run of deeper water.

Your pace in meadow streams should be slower in general. Woodland streams, with their bigger trees in the background, break up your profile and allow you to get closer to the trout. Meadow streams offer little of this natural camouflage, so maintaining a low profile and working slowly is essential for approaching trout without frightening them.

OPPOSITE: The angler pictured here has a good idea on this meadow stream because he's keeping his profile low, but the bright red shirt might not be such great camouflage.

SPRING CREEKS

When fly fishers speak of spring creeks they mean a stream that emerges from the ground at a few relatively large source points, as opposed to streams that are formed by many tiny seeps. (Technically all streams are spring creeks at their headwaters because they all arise from groundwater—otherwise they'd go dry after every rainfall—but we'll stick with the most common nomenclature so you aren't confused when reading other books or talking to other anglers.) To a North American fly fisher, a spring creek is one with a low gradient, constant water temperature, water rich in nutrients, and profuse aquatic weeds. You have to be careful in other countries, though. On a couple trips to Chile, I've been taken to remote "spring creeks" that were more what we'd call a bog, with dark water, no aquatic weeds, and deep flows better fished from a boat than by wading. The definition may lose something in the translation to Spanish, but that's the problem with trying to pigeonhole streams into these unscientific categories. They leave a lot open to interpretation.

Spring creeks are most often found in places with limestone bedrock, especially in the eastern states, but there are exceptions. On many large rivers in the American West, water runs against a bend in the river where hydraulic pressure forces water underground, and on the other side of the bend this water emerges from the ground in what appears to be a spring creek, with no limestone in sight. And in the basalt bedrock of the Northwest, water runs between the hollows in the volcanic bedrock and emerges as a spring at a lower elevation where a fault allows the groundwater to reach the surface.

Spring creeks, whatever their source, grow large trout and, as I said previously, don't really fall into our definition of a small stream except in their very headwaters, where heavy brush or narrow flow causes most anglers to ignore them. But there are ways to catch trout in these tiny springs and if you stick with me you'll learn how to fish them.

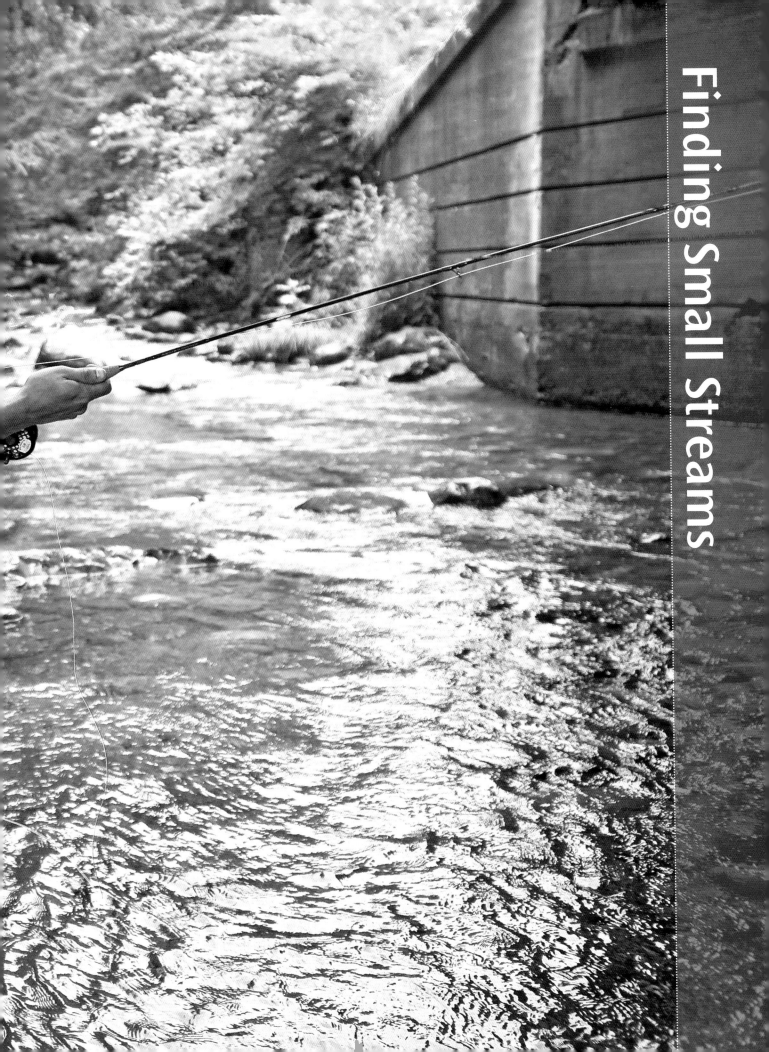

Finding Small Streams

 **Chapter 2** ....

Finding Small Streams

I t's unlikely that you'll find a small stream to fish via conventional means. They don't rate articles in magazines because the fish are too small. Hatches are sparse in most so they don't rate an Internet fishing report. And given their size, most of these streams can't handle a lot of fishing pressure. But that's irrelevant because most anglers, intent on taking photos of bragging-size fish or sitting in a boat while a guide rows them to the best water, have no interest in tiny unknown waters. Hiking a couple of miles through dense brush and scrambling over slippery rocks is not for everyone.

Start with Major Trout Streams

All trout streams have tributaries and the easiest way to find a small stream is by looking for smaller streams that enter a larger river. You already know the area supports trout, and tributaries are used by trout in bigger rivers as spawning areas and cold

water refuges, so you know the small stream has a constant influx of fish. The headwaters of most famous trout streams begin as first-order streams, and often they are completely ignored for lack of parking areas, casting room, or just because no one talks about these spots. Fly fishers will gladly spill the beans about a big trout they've caught, or a major hatch that brought every trout in the river to the surface in an orgy of feeding, and everyone else locks onto these spots. When there are big trout and hatches to match nearby, few people will purposely explore a place where the biggest fish might be eight inches and a Parachute Adams is the only fly you need. Sometimes all you have to do is take a drive upstream along a river until it seems to disappear,

PAGES 40–41: Great small-stream fishing can be found close to civilization if the habitat is healthy.

OPPOSITE: Sometimes it's as much about the journey as the fishing.

Both a traditional paper topographic map and a GPS unit are helpful for finding new streams. The paper map makes it easier to scan wide areas and the GPS gets you within a few feet of the spot.

then look for a line of trees that snakes through a meadow, a gap in the trees, or a dark, narrow canyon. A topographic map is helpful, but a long drive and some dead reckoning will work. Forget about a road atlas or car GPS units. Once a stream dwindles into oblivion people who make road maps lose interest. You'll need to consult the terrain feature on Google maps, a handheld GPS unit with a topographic database, or a plain old paper topo map.

In addition to the headwaters of major streams, you may also find small-stream fishing in tributaries well down on the main river. A careful drive or a few minutes studying a map may help you locate some, but you may also find them as you walk along the banks while fishing. The one piece of advice I can give you is to ignore the first quarter mile or so upstream of a small tributary's junction with the main river. Casual anglers will give these places a few casts as a side trip off the main river, but most won't travel far upstream because they start to feel like they're missing a hatch or a bigger fish on the main river.

One little stream I like to fish is a tributary of a famous trout river and I've never caught a trout closer than 200 yards from the main river. I drive upstream two miles on a small side road, park in a dirt pull-off, and hike for 50 yards to get to the stream.

The brook here has a reputation as a spawning stream for the main river and common knowledge states that the big browns run up in the fall after the season closes. I've seen these big trout in June, six months before spawning, perfectly content to find the deeper pools and logjams where they have likely spent their entire lives. Not that I catch the bigger ones often, as they are so spooky in the thin water that the only sign of them is a tail slinking under a big log as I approach. But if I'm lucky I'll find one rising in the tail of a pool, right before dark, when the water is slightly cloudy from a recent thunderstorm. This happens maybe once every three years, but I keep going back and the little fish offer most of the amusement.

Don't let just a thin trickle of water or impenetrable brush scare you off. Take a hike. As you follow a little tributary upstream, sooner or later you'll find an opening in the brush where you can creep down to the bank and make a short roll cast. Or the canopy may suddenly open into mature forest, where tall trees give you plenty of backcast room straight downstream over the streambed. And just because the water where a brook enters a bigger river is too shallow doesn't mean there won't be a deep plunge pool a mile upstream.

Other Places to Look

Not all small trout streams are tributaries of famous trout waters and thus require greater diligence to find. These are my favorite small streams, because the ones that no one suspects give me the biggest thrill. Because I live in a place where small streams abound (at last count I cross 11 of them on my commute to work each day), I get my greatest pleasure from just discovering a new one, and there are a few that I've only fished once, because after seeing that I could catch trout in a tiny stream that no one ever thought of fishing with a fly, the adventure is gone and I start looking for the next one.

Many of these streams start far up in mountains or hills, separated from major trout streams by scores of miles and joined by so many other streams on their way to a famous river that they get diluted in obscurity. Others begin as springs or in high elevation and run immediately into warm or polluted water so no one even suspects they exist. I have found wild trout within the city limits of many cities in the eastern megalopolis as far south as Roanoke, Virginia, and the writer Monty Montgomery has regaled me with tales of a wild brook trout stream in his neighborhood in suburban Boston. The artist James Prosek has secret wild trout streams in southern Connecticut. And not far from Pasadena is a trout stream that is just far enough into the surrounding hills to stay cold enough for trout. I'm sure it is the same for any city where the groundwater temperature stays under 60 degrees, which should be cold enough for trout to exist year-round, at least close to the source of the stream.

Why 60 degrees? Trout are cold-blooded, and as the temperature in the surrounding water increases their metabolism escalates as well. Problems arise for trout somewhere above 68 degrees, not necessarily because of increased metabolism, but because their oxygen requirements increase. (Remember all that glucose and ATP stuff from high-school biology?) As water warms it can hold less dissolved oxygen, the gas that trout need to pass through their gill filaments. So at high temperatures trout literally burn themselves out, which is why anglers are often advised to quit fishing in high water temperatures. The added energy needed to fight against a fly rod drastically increases a trout's oxygen requirements, and if the water doesn't hold enough oxygen your simple pleasure is lethal to the trout. Trout can live in water

temperatures up to the mid-70s for brief periods as long as they are not stressed, and races of rainbow trout have evolved to survive in even higher water temperatures, but for a healthy trout population, water temperatures should stay below 68 degrees for all but short periods.

Looking at a map of groundwater temperatures will give you a good idea of where to start looking for these secret small streams. The map on the following spread is a rough guide to groundwater temperatures in the United States, and comparing what I know of where small-stream fishing is best to this map, I discovered that you can use the 57-degree line as a reasonably good indicator. North of this line you have a chance of finding a small trout stream almost anywhere water flows off mountains or high hills, or emerges from the ground as springs, especially over places with limestone bedrock.

You can also use elevation as a guideline for locating small trout streams. In the northern United States—approximately anything above 36 degrees north longitude—any streams that begin on the slopes of hills or mountains higher than 2,000 feet have the potential to hold trout. In the mountains of the southeastern United States, the magic altitude is 3,000 feet, and in the hot southwestern United States, in the mountains of Arizona and New Mexico, you have to climb to 6,500 feet. You don't have to fish above these altitudes, just look for the sources of these streams at the higher elevation. You should find water cold enough to hold trout year-round. As the stream you're investigating flows below these altitudes, the length of downstream water that will hold trout depends on the terrain through which the stream flows. Heavily wooded banks and steep valleys keep the heat of the sun off the water longer in the day, and if the stream begins to flow through open meadow or pastureland trout habitat may run out quickly.

Civilization can affect where you find small streams. Suburban sprawl, with its inevitable large expanses of asphalt, will raise summer water temperatures

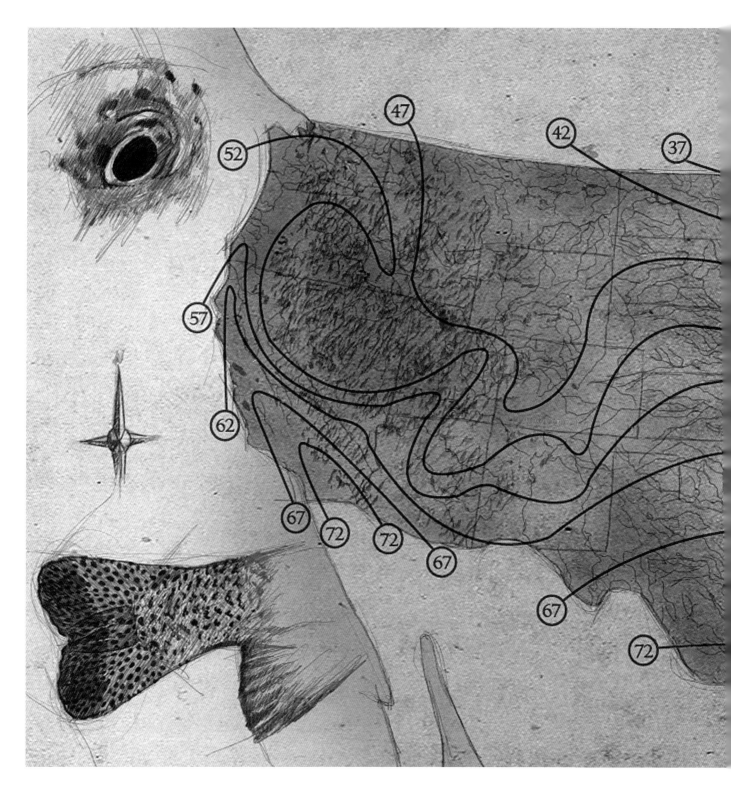

This map shows average groundwater temperatures across the United States. The best small-stream areas are mostly in places with hilly or mountainous terrain where groundwater is a maximum of 62 degrees, but any place spring water rises to the surface in this 62-degree range could harbor small pockets of wild trout.

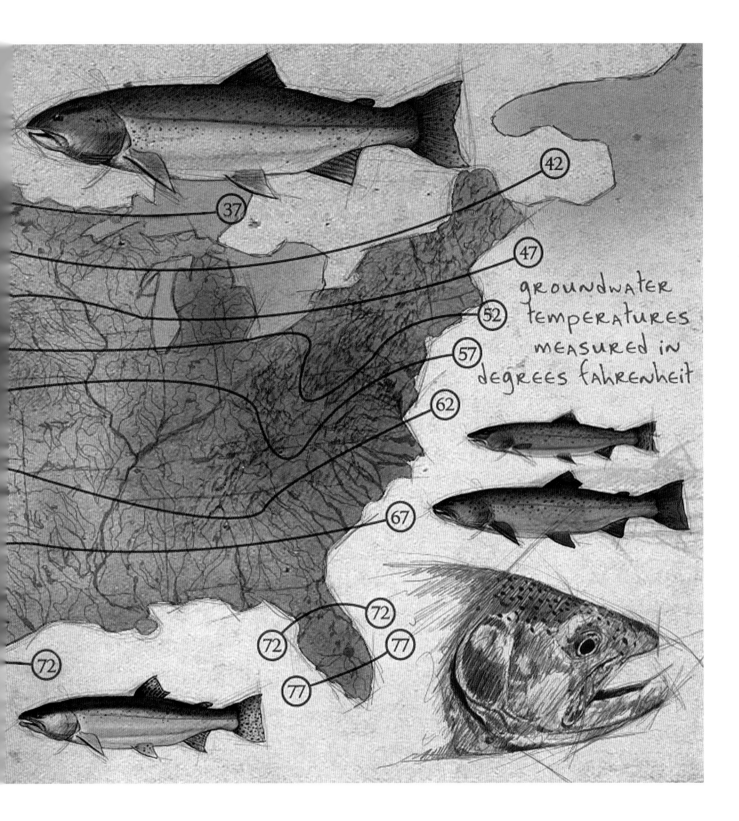

groundwater temperatures measured in degrees fahrenheit

well above what the undeveloped landscape, with vegetation that shades streams and funnels ground-water into the soil, would have done. Monocultures of crops without a strip of riparian trees and shrubs will also raise water temperatures. But civilization can bring a mixed blessing. If water temperatures in small streams that flow through cropland or towns stay below 70 degrees through the summer, nutrients from farm fertilizer and septic systems can enrich the water, increasing the amount of algae in the stream, and thus the amount of trout food available. However, this is a delicate balance, because if the water temperature slips above 70 degrees, the increased algae crop, when it dies, rapidly uses up the available oxygen in a stream through decomposition. So don't give up on small streams just because they flow through populated areas. If you suspect a suburban stream holds trout, just check it with a thermometer during a warm summer day to see if the water temperature is below 70 degrees. I don't know which scenario will draw more stares—a full-grown adult poking through backyards with a fishing rod or running around taking a stream's temperature. That's for you to decide.

Many streams that could not hold trout year-round naturally are stocked by state fish and game departments or municipalities. These streams have water temperatures that will support trout from late fall through early spring, but after the longer days of spring sunshine the water reaches the lethal range for trout. However, stocking times and places are public information, and if you're going to spend the money to stock a stream you want people to know about it, so these streams are seldom secret.

Get Out the Maps and the GPS

Once you've identified a rough location close to your home, or summer place, or vacation destination (after all, the appeal of small-stream fishing is that you don't have to travel hundreds of miles to a famous trout stream to get your fix), it's time to take out the maps and put fresh batteries in the GPS. The best place to start is an old fashioned, plain paper topographic map. You can either order a paper map from the USGS site (store.usgs.gov), or download one and use it on your computer, or print a section yourself. There are also numerous topographic mapping computer software programs available, but they are all based on the USGS data. Google maps work pretty well for locating these streams, but make sure you turn on the "terrain" feature because the standard road-map version misses most small streams. Google Earth and other computer maps based on satellite imagery are not very helpful in locating small streams. Most of the good ones are covered by foliage and even when a small stream runs through an open meadow, the resolution of the satellite map is still not good enough to pinpoint the location. The reason I like a plain paper map is that it's just so much easier to scan a wide area with a paper map as opposed to panning with a GPS unit or a computer program.

Make sure you understand the difference between an intermittent stream (a blue dashed line) and a perennial stream (a solid blue line). You don't want to arrive at your fishing spot to find a dry streambed. Also, learn to recognize the symbols for springs, either a solid blue dot or a blue circle with a squiggly line coming out of it. If you are looking at mountainous country, look above the elevation line that delineates the lower level for trout in your part of the country, and if you are looking at a lower elevation but still somewhere that might hold trout—like the limestone belts in the Midwest—look for streams that begin with the spring symbol.

Contour lines on maps can help you determine what type of water to expect even from the comfort of your living room. Streams with dense contour lines along their course means canyon water, which will typically be fast pocket water or steep waterfalls with interesting plunge pools below them. Beware of first-order streams with dense contour lines where the lines never cross the stream, or

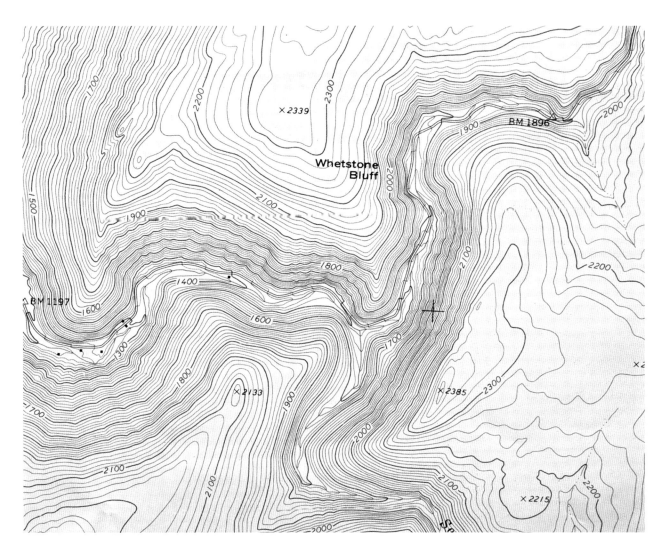

This spot on a topographic map would be intriguing: steep valley walls that keep the stream shaded, a number of bends that indicate deeper pools, and a small third-order stream coming in from the south. A small secondary road would make access easy as well.

where they are dense throughout its length. A stream like this might be impossible to fish and may not have enough quiet water to hold fish. I like to see dense contours punctuated by more open sections where the contours cross the stream, which means the canyon has opened up into a little plateau or meadow where the stream might tarry long enough to form a nice pool.

Whether you look close to roads or trails depends on your constitution. Streams located right alongside a road are probably more heavily fished by locals who know the area, but they can still be quite

good and because of their tiny size may be ignored by most people. When Scott Farfone took me to a couple of his favorite brook trout streams in the Blue Ridge Mountains of North Carolina, I expected we'd be hiking a few miles into the mountains. But one of these streams was right next to the road, and another was paralleled by a hiking trail with a steady procession of kids in sneakers and tourists walking fluffy little white dogs that looked more like bait than pets.

The real gems, however, may be off the grid. At lower altitudes, look for streams that originate as springs or ones that begin in between areas of steep contours that indicate a partially shaded valley. At higher altitudes, streams that originate in lakes may be productive trout waters, but below 4,000 to 6,000 feet (depending on where you are) lakes at the headwaters of a stream can make the water too warm for trout. I like to look for a first-order stream that has at least a couple of additional first-order streams running into it. This gives me the opportunity to explore one larger stream plus a couple of smaller ones in a single area.

Also look for stream courses that are more like wiggly blue lines than straight shots. The more bends in a small stream, the greater the number of pools; streams always dig holes where they encounter a change in direction. A straight piece of water on the map might be a nice section of pocket water when you see it for real, but it might also be a long boring riffle or a swift cascade with no respite from the current for trout to live.

I transfer the coordinates, or just eyeball the location, and find it on the screen of a GPS unit with preloaded topographic maps, like the Garmin Oregon 400t. If you're adept with a map and compass you can forgo the GPS, but I find these units so much more useful in the field than paper maps and compasses. After transferring the coordinates, I drive to the nearest vehicle access point (using my car GPS unit—I really love these gadgets) and route to the waypoint, keeping steep contour lines in mind so that I can avoid really steep hills if possible.

Learn to identify the way private land is marked in the state where you are fishing, and how stream access laws work, because every state is different. In Montana, if you can access a stream from a public right-of-way, you can follow the stream up to its headwaters, even through private land, as long as you stay in the stream or along its immediate banks to the high-water mark. You are even allowed to go around obstructions if they impede your upstream progress. In Colorado and New York, the landowner owns the bed of the river, and if both banks are posted as private land, you cannot wade up through a stream without permission. The various states even

Read posted signs carefully. It's always best to ask permission to fish private land, but chances are it's fine with this landowner.

have their own ways of posting private land. In Wyoming, fence posts every 600 feet painted in fluorescent orange indicate private land, and crossing one of these fences might earn you a stern warning or worse. In many states, land must be posted with signs of a certain size and at a required minimum interval, but you don't really want to argue with a landowner about whether he or she has followed the letter of the law. You should read these signs carefully, however, because sometimes just seeing a posted sign from a speeding car might not tell you the whole story. In Vermont, for instance, you frequently see posted signs that state "No hunting, shooting, or trapping," which means that it's perfectly OK to trespass to fish as long as you respect the landowner's property. And because most posted signs must be signed with the landowner's name, a little legwork might get you permission to fish a stream that has everyone else scared off because they didn't take the time to ask a landowner politely.

Of course you can avoid all this by limiting your fishing expeditions on small streams to Forest Service or National Forest land, public parks of other types, State Wildlife Management Areas, or Bureau of Land Management (BLM) land. Most states offer maps online that indicate stretches of public land, so you can include this information when planning your small-stream journey.

Best Small-Stream Places in the United States

Some regions of the United States are packed with hundreds of unknown streams just waiting to be discovered. In places like Vermont and Montana and the Cascades of the Northwest, virtually every piece of moving water holds at least a small population of trout. In Vermont, where I've lived for the past 33 years, we're blessed with abundant springs and mountains high enough to supply cold groundwater throughout the year. The state is also not highly developed, which keeps waters colder and more pure than in suburban areas. I have yet to find one perennial stream in the state that does not hold at least a sparse population of miniature brook trout in its headwaters, and I'm sure that in other parts of the country where groundwater is cool enough, the adventurous angler is blessed with similar opportunities.

Brook trout are superbly adapted to colonizing headwater streams and can live in places that support no other fish, but they are highly susceptible to warm water with low dissolved oxygen.

Mountain streams in New England are usually infertile, which means small trout will grab nearly any fly that looks remotely edible.

The regions below are those that host an abundance of tiny streams. There are isolated trout streams in other parts of the country as well, wherever cold springs emerge from the ground and stay cool for at least a mile, but the regions I've listed are those where even the visiting angler, with a few hours of research and a day to explore, can find productive small-stream fishing.

When you want to target a particular species of trout in your explorations, it's important to recognize the change in fish populations that occurs in most small streams. In the lower reaches of most small streams in the East, the farthest from their source, the water is warmer and the food supply is richer. Here you'll find brown and rainbow trout, sometimes mixed with brook trout, plus small fish like dace, darters, and sculpins. But as you ascend in altitude and get closer to the source of a stream, you'll find mostly brook trout, even in streams with no lower barrier impassable to fish. And when you get very close to the headwaters even the small baitfish are absent, leaving only brook trout. Why? As you get closer to the source of a stream the acidity of the water increases, and brook trout are far more tolerant of acid waters than browns or rainbows. In fact, biologist Bob Bachman found that brook trout acclimated to highly acidic waters in headwater streams, when transplanted to "better," more alkaline water, actually died. The water here is also cold year-round, below 60 degrees, and browns and rainbows prefer water temperatures of 55 to 65 degrees because they cannot grow efficiently in colder water temperatures. Aquatic insects are also very sparse in headwaters, but the brook trout have adapted to subsisting entirely on terrestrial insects, which are too big for the smaller baitfish to inhale.

Brook trout are what Bachman calls a "weed species," which makes most small-stream anglers cringe because we are so in love with the fish. But the definition of a weed species is a plant that can grow in conditions too harsh for other plants, and brook trout are highly adapted to the very harsh environments found in headwater streams—constant low temperatures that rainbows and browns avoid, high acidity, and an unpredictable food supply. Although it's true that browns and rainbows often outcompete brook trout for habitat and food, brook trout have another, more serious problem at lower elevations. They are very intolerant of low dissolved oxygen levels, and where we often blame the invasive brown and rainbow trout for the decline of brook trout populations, we should probably blame ourselves as well for logging and developing the lower reaches of these streams, raising the water temperatures, and thus lowering the dissolved oxygen content.

You'll find a similar scenario on western small streams, with browns and rainbows at lower elevations and cutthroats, golden trout, Gila trout, and Apache trout at higher altitudes. Here it's not so much a matter of acidity, as rainwater in the West is not as acidic, but the cutthroats and the rare headwater species do survive better in the colder water and inconsistent food supply found at higher altitudes. Brook trout have also been introduced in the West, where they may invade headwater streams beside the native species.

▪ THE NORTHEAST

The great Northeast, in which I include northern Maine, the Canadian Maritime provinces, and northern Ontario and Quebec, is full of small brook trout streams, mostly low-gradient boggy ones that are ignored by anglers looking for trophy trout or landlocked salmon. This infertile country, characterized by vast expanses of black spruce and granite bedrock, supports mostly acidic streams. Because the native brook trout are more acid-tolerant than the introduced browns and rainbows, you will find browns and rainbows only in the lower reaches of streams that run into richer valleys. When I was a kid I often took vacations to New Brunswick and Nova Scotia with my parents, and because I was scared of the bigger salmon rivers and felt my little trout rod and my experience were inadequate, I'd find the closest tea-stained brook to our campsite each night. And I always caught at least a few brook trout. They were hardly big enough to put a bend in my stiff, blue fiberglass rod, but each one stirred my teenage soul.

The White Mountains of northern New Hampshire, the Adirondacks of New York, and most of Vermont—except for the Lake Champlain Valley—are full of tiny streams. They range from boggy, lowland streams linking beaver ponds to rushing mountain streams dumping off the slopes of the low, rounded mountains. Northern Vermont and New Hampshire, as well as the central Green Mountain spine of Vermont and the Adirondacks, are brook trout waters, with, as usual, a mix of browns and rainbows in their lower reaches. Southwestern Vermont is influenced by the Taconic Mountains, which extend down through the Berkshires of Massachusetts and along the Hudson River Valley of New York. The bedrock underlying these mountains is more alkaline than the rest of the northeastern mountains, and with lower acidity and a richer food supply you can find wild browns and rainbows as well as brook trout in tiny streams in this region. The Catskill Mountains of New York, famous for bigger trout streams like the Beaverkill, Delaware, and Esopus, hide many tiny streams never even considered by the armies of fly fishers who venture north from the New York metropolitan area each weekend. Some of these streams are tributaries of the famous rivers and hold wild browns and rainbows in their lower reaches and brook trout in their headwaters. Others are tiny acidic streams high in the mountains on National Forest land and are dominated by tiny brook trout. Every time I visit the heavily fished Beaverkill I always spend an hour

Brown trout can tolerate warmer water temperatures than brook trout, but they require a richer food supply to thrive. Thus, they are more often found farther downstream than brook trout.

or two on a little tributary to get away from the crowds. The brook trout are tiny and not very numerous, but they're wild fish in a lush deciduous cathedral and I've never seen another angler there.

■ THE MID-ATLANTIC AND THE SOUTHEAST

Pennsylvania is small-stream heaven, and unlike many other places, the anglers there are savvy to its pleasures. It has a long tradition of small-stream experts like the legendary Joe Humphreys, who I once saw fire a bow-and-arrow cast 30 feet, driving his fly underneath a parked car. (You'll learn about the bow-and-arrow cast in Chapter Six, but it's a cast that most anglers use just to cast the length of a rod.) You'll find most of the small-stream fishing in the Allegheny Mountains in the north and center of the state, but because much of Pennsylvania lies over limestone bedrock, tiny spring creeks pop up in many unexpected places, especially in the Cumberland Valley in the southeastern part of the state. The Alleghenies are full of slate-bottomed, rhododendron-lined streams that run cold and clear all

summer long. This fishing extends south to West Virginia and northwestern Maryland.

The entire spine of the Great Smoky Mountains offers some of the finest small-stream fishing in the East. The cool summers and relatively mild winters, along with abundant mountain springs, ensure that a fly fisher can catch trout in the heat of summer above 4,000 feet, but can also catch trout all winter long. I've had some of my most enjoyable small-stream fishing for wild brook trout in this region a half-hour from downtown Roanoke, Virginia, and in northwestern North Carolina. The fishing extends south to the northwest tip of South Carolina into northern Georgia, where wild native brook trout can still be found, along with introduced browns and rainbows.

■ THE MIDWEST

As you work west, Ohio has a few small streams that emerge from springs in limestone bedrock in the Grand and Chagrin river systems, but some of these streams hold rare and protected populations of wild brook trout and fishing is prohibited. The

Upper Peninsula of Michigan, northern Wisconsin, and the Arrowhead Region of northern Minnesota along the western shore of Lake Superior are filled with small brook trout streams that seldom get fished. The lower peninsula of Michigan, particularly from the center of the state to the west coast of Lake Huron, is full of brook trout streams that are cold, sand-bottomed streams that run through tag alder and cedar swamps. This is rugged country and not easy to negotiate, so most of the small streams are ignored except by early-season worm anglers.

But the lowland in the Midwest also offers surprises. In the corner where Wisconsin, Illinois, and Iowa meet is a special area of unglaciated land called the Driftless Region, where cold limestone springs emerge in the hilly farmland and trout—even wild brook trout—prosper. These streams flow into larger streams that eventually dump into the Mississippi, and the area is defined by a line from Rochester to Redwing, Minnesota, and down through northeastern Iowa and southeastern Wisconsin. Some of these streams like the Kickapoo and Root River are well-known, but the area also hosts many tiny streams off the radar screen of most fly fishers. Further south, southern Missouri and northern Arkansas have limestone springs that feed tiny wild trout streams in the Ozark Mountains. The Black Hills of South Dakota are also high enough to form trout streams. The region contains more than 1,200 miles of trout streams, most of them small, and they range from mountain freestone streams to valley spring creeks.

■ THE ROCKIES

And, of course, all of the Rocky Mountains—Alberta and British Colombia, through eastern Montana and the Idaho panhandle, down through Wyoming and Colorado and into Arizona and New Mexico—have some of the best small-stream fishing in the world. With high altitudes, many springs, and vast parcels of public land, the small-stream angler could happily exist in just one small grid in any of these states. An added attraction is that the larger trout rivers in this part of the world are so good that the small streams are guaranteed to be ignored. I was once staying at a fly-fishing lodge on the Madison River and asked the manager if anyone ever fished the little stream that ran under the driveway on the road into the ranch. The manager told me no one had fished it since last year, which of course was like waving a red flag in front of a bull. I pushed down through some thick patches of Russian olive and negotiated a few barbed-wire fences until I was a half mile or so below the ranch, and spent the next two hours working my way upstream, slowly picking each pocket with a size 14 Yellow Humpy. I never count fish, but I must have caught around 40 trout in those two hours, none of them monsters, but some that took enough line to get me worried about snagging my leader on logjams. I won't say the fish were stupid, but they sure made me feel like a hero.

In the hotter high-desert regions of southern Colorado, you begin to encounter the 6,500-foot elevation rule, which holds as you descend into the mountain trout streams of the Sangre de Cristo, Pecos, and Gila Mountains of northern New Mexico, as well as the White Mountains of eastern Arizona. Here you'll find the usual browns and rainbows lower in the creeks, with cutthroats and brook trout at the higher elevations. If you're lucky, you may catch and carefully release the rare and threatened Gila trout in the Gila National Forest of New Mexico and the Apache trout in the White Mountains of Arizona. (You should always check current regulations. At the time I was writing this, a special free permit was required to fish for Gila trout.) Both of these species are adapted to thriving in the high-altitude headwater creeks of the southwest, just the kind of fishing we'll explore in this book.

Utah also has excellent small-stream fishing in creeks that run off the Wasatch Mountains in the center of the state, and the more remote Uinta Mountains of eastern Utah. You don't think of trout fishing in Utah outside of the famous Green and Provo rivers, but I've had wonderful small-stream fishing in this state, from a cute little stream that runs right through downtown Park City to gorgeous high-mountain streams that run through spectacular aspen groves above 7,000 feet in the Uintas.

◼ THE WEST COAST

On the West Coast, steelhead and large resident rainbows and browns get all the glory, but where there are large trout streams you'll always find great small-stream fishing. The coastal range from southern Washington to northern California is full of small

OPPOSITE: Because the Rocky Mountains contain so many famous and productive rivers, the small streams in this region get little fishing pressure.

creeks that hold resident populations of tiny cutthroats, and the lower reaches of these streams in the foothills sometimes offer runs of sea-run cutthroats which can grow much bigger. Juvenile steelhead and salmon are present in many of these streams, and because some are important as spawning streams they may be closed to fishing part of the season.

The Cascade Range offers the best small-stream opportunities in the Northwest. The streams are wetter and more acidic, which means a sparser food supply, and trout here are smaller but less fussy about what fly pattern they take. The western Cascades are drier with less vegetation, but have richer, more alkaline waters and larger trout. Native cutthroats and rainbows are most common in the Cascades, with some introduced brook trout at higher elevations.

Cutthroat trout are the native headwater species in most western states.

Rainbow trout are native to Pacific drainage streams, but have been stocked throughout the world. They can live and feed in faster water than any other trout species.

The Sierras, particularly at higher elevations, offer spectacular small-stream trout fishing on the eastern slopes, where mountain slopes rise from the floor of the Mojave Desert at 4,000 feet to high granite escarpments of up to 14,000 feet in just a few miles. As a result, the streams are mostly rushing, high-gradient streams with a sparse food supply and the fish are eager to take almost any fly pattern at will. Here you'll find native cutthroats as well as California's other native fish, the rare golden trout, which can be found in small streams in the Golden Trout Wilderness Area at the headwaters of the Kern River. Introduced rainbow, brown, and brook trout are also common in these high-altitude streams because they have been stocked in many of the alpine lakes in the region. Most of the fishing emphasis in this region is on lakes, where the bigger trout grow, which means the small streams are largely ignored except for those which hold golden trout, which, in its native habitat, is a rare prize for a fly fisher.

This is not a guidebook to small streams of the United States. A great deal of the pleasure in fishing these streams is discovering them, and if I included them in this book it would take away much of your fun. Plus, I'd probably have a bunch of people with sporting art in their living rooms putting a contract out on me, and I'd like to live to a ripe old age so I can discover lots more tiny streams with my son. I've given you some strong hints on where to find them. Now we'll spend some time exploring techniques on how to fish them.

OPPOSITE: Little streams like this are sensitive to fishing pressure and it's best if they are not heavily publicized.

Chapter 3

Reading the Water and Finding Trout in Small Streams

When I'm asked to do a seminar or a podcast, a common request is a program on reading the water. I think some anglers hope that somewhere in the quagmire of fly-fishing books and articles is a standard manual on reading the water, a long-forgotten volume on the secrets to this black art. If you're looking for specific rules, such as, "When a big, flat rock is above a round rock, trout will always be found on the left side of the round rock," I think you will live an unfulfilled life. Reading the water is a dynamic skill that changes with water levels, kinds of food, amount of fishing pressure, and the quantity and species of predators that threaten a trout population. It

also depends greatly on an invisible force that is perhaps the most important aspect of reading the water: fluid hydraulics.

Water, Friction, and Turbulence

Water flow is either classified as laminar or turbulent. True laminar flow, where the water flows straight downstream without any diversion in direction, is virtually nonexistent in trout streams. Any tiny projection in the bank, on the streambed, or any change in direction causes friction, which changes the direction of the flow and slows its downstream progress. It's this turbulence that forms slow pockets in the current where trout can rest and feed. The larger the irregularities and their density, the greater the turbulence and the more places for a trout to live. So when looking over a small stream, those with more rocks on the bottom, or more logs or large rocks along the bank, will potentially hold more trout.

PAGES 62–63: Trout will probably not be found in the standing wave in the middle of this little pool, but they could be in the clear lenses on either side of it.

OPPOSITE: Just a bit of elevation above water level can give you a much better look at the structure in a pool.

There is a point where turbulence gets too strong and trout have trouble holding in the current because they can't maintain their position. When you see smooth whirling cells of water that change shape constantly and boil from the bottom, making large bulges in the surface, the water is too turbulent. In extreme cases—especially in very fast current with hydraulic jump (places that exhibit a very quick change in slope, releasing potential energy and causing extreme turbulent mixing)—standing waves might form. In this water, a trout's food gets pushed aside unpredictably and fish don't like food snatched from their jaws just when they think they're about to get a mouthful. Besides, they have trouble holding their position when being pushed from different directions at once. Better turbulence is found when the water shows a gentle riffle that moves in a predictable direction—it might be the edge of a whirlpool that moves upstream, a finger of current that is suddenly pushed sideways, or a gentle, dimpled run that flows at a stately pace downstream. As long as the flow is predictable, trout are content.

Friction causes turbulence behind objects and along their sides, but a less intuitive aspect is that turbulence will also develop in front of an object. When current hits an obstruction dead-on, it bounces back and the loss of energy is transferred back a longer distance than you might think, forming a cushion or pillow in front of a rock or log. In addition, the turbulence that forms in front of an object digs out the gravel or sand in front of a rock and forms a deeper pocket, which provides additional protection from the current.

Often the spots where turbulence is just right are immediately apparent to humans peering through the surface. Pockets around large rocks, places where a shallow riffle suddenly dumps into a deep pool, and logs that stretch out into the current are obvious places to find trout, as they offer protection from the current and a place to hide when danger looms. However, because actual hydraulics are invisible to us, we only see their obvious manifesta-tions on the surface. We can't see, for instance, what happens when the turbulence between a set of underwater rocks converges, which is why a trout will occupy one place on the bottom that looks just OK and not another spot in the pool that looks terrific. We just can't see what's going on, so we have to rely upon those few gross changes we *can* see on the surface—plus a lot of experience and guesswork. Reading the water is not an exact science.

Spotting Trout

Trout are mostly invisible to us, even when they are in shallow water. Their spot patterns act as superb camouflage, and their skin also has the ability to change to a lighter or darker shade in a matter of hours, so not only is their profile broken up, but it will also match the shade of the river bottom. Nevertheless, reading the water begins with attempting to spot trout in the water. If you can see a trout in the water you have a much better chance of catching it, and observing how a trout uses the current and bottom structure will give you a leg up when fishing water where they can't be seen.

When spotting trout, you hardly ever see the entire fish at first. You see a fin that suddenly morphs into a back and then a head, or you notice a thin rock edge that seems to sway back and forth when the other rock edges on the bottom are motionless. One of the best ways to spot a trout is by its shadow, because a trout's body is well camouflaged, but its shadow is a sharp-edged black form. However, to get a shadow you need bright sunlight and the trout must be suspended above the bottom somewhat, so this mainly helps you spot trout when they are in slower water, suspended above the bottom, feeding on the surface or in mid-water. A trout resting on the bottom on a cloudy day does not throw much of a shadow.

Trout look different in every kind of water they inhabit, and different species may vary in shade. Brown trout often look, well, brown or sometimes yellow in the water. Cutthroats are pinkish with shades of orange. Rainbows are gray or light blue, and brook trout are greenish blue. At least that's how my eyes see them. So it takes a while to pick up a search image that includes both the shade and shape of a trout. When I'm hunting for wild mushrooms in the summer and bright, flat-shaped yellowish orange chanterelles are abundant, I might walk right past a patch of shorter, pitcher-shaped black trumpets, but if I was looking for black trumpets I'd never miss them.

One of the best ways to learn to spot trout is to catch one first. It's easy for me to say, I know, but once you catch a trout and revive it in shallow water, don't just look up for another riser once you release the fish. Follow it carefully back through the shallow water. Often a released trout, once it reaches a riffle or slightly deeper water where it feels more secure, will stop and rest further. Watch that fish like an osprey, and remember its shape and shade. It will help you be able to identify them later.

What Trout Need

I get annoyed when I write about trout fishing because I find myself overusing waffling adverbs like "sometimes" and "often." But trout are wild creatures and encompass three genera (*Salmo, Onchorynchus, and Salvelinus*), and inhabit streams of all shapes and sizes. They even have individual personalities, and a trout on one side of a tiny pool might behave differently than his buddy on the other side of a rock. So giving you concrete rules for reading the water is foolish. I think it's better to understand what trout need, how they feed, and how currents affect them. Of course I'll give you some hints, but I think they'll make more sense if you spend some time learning

Trout are superbly camouflaged. Without this trout's tail silhouetted against the submerged log, it would be very tough to spot, and every little distortion in the surface of the water makes the trout more difficult to see.

details that you can use on any small trout stream, anywhere in the world.

In most large trout streams there are two kinds of feeding behavior. Most trout are drift feeders, which means they station themselves in a safe, comfortable place in a stream and pluck food from the current as it drifts by. But a few individuals in each stretch of water, usually the bigger ones—fish longer than 14 inches (or perhaps 20 inches in very food-rich streams where the fish grow bigger on average)—develop a hunting, ambushing strategy where they feed less often, but cruise through a pool hunting for bigger prey like baitfish, crayfish, mice, or frogs. They act more like pike than trout. You might find these hunters eating insects during a heavy hatch, but if food in the current is not abundant they'll rest under heavy cover for days at a time, only leaving the security of a logjam or deep pool after dark or when a rainstorm clouds the water and makes hunting baitfish easier. In small streams we seldom find these bigger hunters. Baitfish and crayfish are not abundant in first- or second-order streams, so we should concentrate on drift-feeding trout when planning our strategy in small streams.

Drift-feeding trout like to lie in water that flows at about one foot per second and lies adjacent to water that is slightly faster. Move your finger in front of your face a foot while you say "one-thousand-one." This piece of one-foot-per-second water does not have to be very large—it can be just slightly wider and longer than a trout's body, so a little depression in a riffle or a slight projection where the current slams against a rocky bank may be enough to give a trout a comfortable place to lie and feed.

Trout are not territorial in the way behavioral scientists describe this behavior, because a territorial animal defends a specific location, and although a

trout may spend 90 percent of its time in one spot, many of them have three or four different places within a pool. A trout may lie on the edge of the fast current when food is scarce and it needs the visual protection from predators that the wrinkled, distorted surface of fast water gives it. When insects are hatching, this same fish might slide back to the tail of the pool, where it can see floating insects better against the smooth surface, and where the current (and thus drifting food) is constricted both horizontally and vertically. When frightened by an angler or otter, this same fish will always have a bolt-hole like a logjam or deep pocket beneath a piece of flat rock where it can swim quickly to get out of danger. This fish will not defend a territory, but if it is larger than other fish or more aggressive, it will defend its immediate location, especially in front of it. Trout that move up behind this trout, or are visually isolated from the trout by a rock or bubbles in the current, will be ignored and you can often find pockets of fish in one place feeding quite close together. The biggest one will almost always take the upstream position. In general, the greater the number of rocks or other obstacles in a pool, the greater the number of trout you'll find living and feeding there.

The Importance of Cover and Shade

When I give a seminar on reading the water, I always ask, "What is the most important need of a trout, assuming water temperature and oxygen are within a comfortable range?" And the most common answer is always, "Cover!" But that's not correct. The most important need is getting enough food while lying in a current that won't burn all the calories the fish is consuming while feeding. Trout will forgo secure protection if it's not right beside a good place to feed, because all the protection in the world won't help if they starve. Now there are many places where trout can find that one-foot-per-second flow alongside faster current and still be hidden next to a log or large rock, and these are often known as "prime lies," as opposed to "feeding lies" or "protection lies." (A feeding lie is one that a trout uses only for eating, returning to a more protected location after it finishes gorging. A protection lie is that logjam in the bottom of a deep pool where a trout hides when disturbed or when it is not eating.) A prime lie affords everything a trout needs without having to move, and these are the places most anglers concentrate on, for good reason. Prime lies often (there goes that indecisive word again) hold the largest fish in a pool. But for every prime lie in a pool, there are a half dozen lies that are perfect feeding lies. The problem is that fish in feeding lies are often more spooky, less secure, than fish feeding out in the open because the current there is perfect. Additionally, a trout in a prime lie will many times be visually isolated from an approaching angler because the rock or log that provides shelter often hides your approach.

I shouldn't imply that cover is not important to small-stream trout; it's essential. If you compare two stretches of a small stream, one with wide-open gravel and no streamside brush and one pocked with boulders and logs, the stretch with the greater density of cover will hold more fish. Trout in small streams are, by definition, almost always living in shallow water, and where trout in rivers have deep pools and large expanses of riffles where distortion on the surface hides the fish from predators, trout in small streams don't have the same luxury. Otters can swim across a small stream with one wiggle of their torso. Raccoons can swipe at trout without getting their feet wet. Kingfishers can see to the bottom of every pool.

Shade is another form of cover. Less light getting into the water means trout shadows are not as visible, and if the foliage causing the shade is low to the water it prevents avian predators like ospreys and kingfishers from diving on trout from a perch above. But I think many anglers overemphasize the importance of shade. It changes throughout the day, and a trout is reluctant

to move into shade that does not also offer a steady food supply. Although there is no doubt that trout feed more aggressively on cloudy days, in the morning before the sun hits the water, and in the evening after the sun is off the water, I think this is more a response to insect abundance, as most aquatic insects hatch more readily in low light than in bright sunlight. Trout can and will feed in bright sunlight if they are not disturbed and food is present. So pay attention to shaded areas of a small stream, but also keep an eye on current threads and where food is drifting. Shade does amplify the possibility of trout being in a spot if the main current threads pass through the shade.

Tim Romano pulls a nice cutthroat from the seam alongside the fast water at the head of this pool.

But when fishing a small stream, don't just look right next to cover to find fish. Use the presence or absence of cover to find the right *part* of a small stream to fish. Then use your knowledge of how water flows through a tiny pool to look for places they'll be eating.

Learn to Find the Thalweg

Stream ecologists and hydrologists use the term "thalweg" to describe the deepest part of the channel that runs through a pool, which usually hosts the fastest current and carries the most debris—

and food. Anglers call this the "bubble line" because you can trace its passage as it winds through a pool by the line of bubbles or foam that betrays its progress. Because most small streams have relatively slow current as compared to bigger rivers, and their food supply is also sparse, finding this line is one of the most important tools in learning to read the water. You may see a fishy-looking log on one side of a pool that you're sure will hold trout, but if the main thread of current misses the log by five feet, you might find trout hiding there when they are frightened, but probably not when they are feeding. One way to eliminate spots in a

pool where you *won't* find trout is to look for leaves and other lightweight debris on the bottom. If the current is slow enough to accumulate lightweight debris, it's probably too slow to bring sufficient food to a hungry trout.

Get a Wider View of Your Stream

When reading the water, we often get too involved in staring at a particular rock or log and forget about a small stream as a long, continuous habitat with some spots much better than others. Trout abundance is often spotty, and the beauty of fishing a small stream is that you probably won't have any competition for the pools so you can walk a half mile to find a better spot. For instance, I've often found that the best-looking, deepest pools are not always the places I catch the best or the most trout. Sometimes these tasty spots get fished hard by casual anglers, who tend to keep fish more often than serious fly fishers. Bait and spin anglers in particular have a much easier time in bigger pools and they usually keep more fish than people using flies. Deep, dark pools may also harbor a single large brown trout that might only feed once or twice a week when it comes out from the depths to spear a minnow or crayfish. Close to civilization, a pool with enough water to jump into without cracking your head might be a swimming hole that was full of splashing kids an hour ago, sending all the trout to the depths to huddle in fright for hours. Keep an eye out for rope swings.

In a small mountain stream with a steep gradient, try to step back and get a look at as large an expanse of stream as you can. Look at the slope of the land, and look for plateaus in the slope where the water will get a little slower and deeper than in the fast cascades. This is especially important in small streams, where the riffles and cascades between pools may be too shallow to hold fish. Trout will hold and feed in water as shallow as six inches, but they also need a deeper refuge close by.

Given a choice of a straight piece of river and one that meanders back and forth, you should always head for the curvy water. It might be tougher to cast in a tight bend because you don't have an alley of backcast room in front of and behind you, but bends in a stream always create at least deeper pockets and often true pools. Current hitting a bend in a river is faster on the outside, so it digs a channel on the fast side and deposits sand and gravel on the slower inside seam. When water hits a bend in a stream with grass, brush, or trees right up to the bank, the current digs an undercut that provides superb shelter against predators.

Don't let a seemingly impassable waterfall scare you away from exploring farther upstream on tiny creeks. First, the stream beyond the falls may be stocked with hatchery fish. Even if you prefer fishing for wild trout, it might have been stocked years ago and could now hold a reproducing population of wild trout. But even if you know the location has never been stocked, trout could still be above that waterfall. At high-water flows, there are often side channels that flow around the obstruction. And did you know that a trout can jump a vertical obstruction *seven times* its body length? This means that a nine-inch trout can jump a five-foot waterfall, maybe even more, because the velocity of water at the top of a waterfall is always less than that at the bottom, and if the waterfall isn't completely vertical, a trout can jump partway up the falls and swim the rest of the way.

Even streams that go dry in places can hold trout, living in spring-fed pools without any current until higher flows bring water back into the channel. My friend Bob Bachman, who holds a Ph.D. in trout behavior and was head of both the Maryland Department of Freshwater Fisheries and the Pennsylvania Fish Commission before he retired, has dug healthy brook trout out of gravel that was dry on the surface but had a subterranean flow. So never assume a tiny stream does not have trout until you've fished it. Between waterfalls and a trout's ability to tolerate extremely low flows like this, a bigger problem—as experienced by fisheries managers trying to keep invasive rainbow and brown trout from the headwaters of native brook trout and cutthroat streams—is trying to keep the non-native trout *out* of headwater streams.

Specific Stream-Reading Tips

Now we get down to the details of what I'll bet you thought reading the water in small streams was all about: locating fish in relation to rocks and logs and undercut banks. You should take heart in that reading the water in a small stream is much easier than reading the water in a big river. Trout distribution in moving water is never uniform. Some places will be full of trout, some will have a few widely scattered individuals, and many places in trout streams are completely barren of fish—or they might hold three-inch young-of-the-year fish only. In a small stream, the distance between a spot that holds fish and one that doesn't might be only a foot, and because trout in small streams don't get the same bountiful food supply as fish in bigger rivers, they are more inclined to move a foot or so for a fly, whereas trout in bigger rivers, where they are well fed, might not move more than a few inches for a fly. In a big river you might have to walk a half mile between spots that hold fish!

But that does not mean you can get sloppy in your stream-reading skills. While it's possible to cover a tiny pool with just a few casts, by casting blindly to cover all the water you risk dumping your fly line on top of a trout, which is sure to scare it

By watching where the bubbles progress through a pool, Bill Reed can predict trout feeding spots. Notice that the bubbles stay closer to the right bank than the left, so when he starts casting in this pool he places most of his casts from the center to the right bank.

Eric Rickstad hooks this fish in a prime lie—in the shade, in the deepest part of the tiny pool, right next to the main current, and alongside a fallen log.

and keep it from feeding for a few minutes to a few hours, depending on how much you frighten it. By making precise casts only to places where you suspect trout will be lying, you will have many more opportunities to put just your fly and tippet over a feeding fish. In addition, drag is often a big problem in small streams, especially in the tails of pools or where conflicting currents snatch a fly out of the current it is drifting in. Again, by making precise casts you will get a short, drag-free, effective float over places where trout are feeding.

■ DEPTH, LOGS, BENDS, AND ROCKS

Depth is usually a limiting factor in where trout live in small streams. The deeper pools and pockets will usually hold the most fish. A big plunge pool beneath a waterfall is an obvious place where you'll find this depth, but some small streams have few well-defined pools and you have to look closer. In one small stream I was fishing on my lunch hour while researching this book, I caught a respectable 11-inch brown trout from a shallow run. Something told me right where he would be and I was right, but I stopped fishing for a few minutes and reflected on why I just knew a good fish would be lying in that spot, as it was not immediately next to the two large rocks in the run. I realized that the fish was holding in the one spot in the pool where the bottom was blurry, where I could not see sharp contrast between the edges of the rocks. It was the deepest slot in the pool, and I now use this method in very shallow water to help me find the deepest water. I find the spot where the bottom just begins to get blurry, knowing that I'll be fishing the deepest part.

Everyone wants to learn about finding trout in relation to rocks in the streambed. Trout hang in the slow current behind a rock, as long as it is not so

In a tiny stream like this one, depth will be the limiting factor. Look for the deepest pockets—the spots where the bottom starts to blur.

turbulent that the currents swirl in all directions, and as long as the rock is not too large, over a few feet across. The reason trout will not be found as often behind very large rocks is that they block all the drifting food from the place immediately behind them, and although the current speed right behind the rock may be very comfortable for a trout, if that rock strains all the food off to either side a trout living there will starve. In the case of large rocks, trout will more often be found along its sides or directly in front of it.

In fact, especially in small streams, the spot in front of a rock is almost always a better spot than behind a rock. Because food is at a premium, trout take up positions where they will encounter the greatest amount of drifting food, and they also like to be able to see the food coming toward them while keeping

an eye out for predators. The view is much better in front of a rock, and the front of a rock is a gourmet deli compared to the soup kitchen behind it. Don't just look for trout in relation to single rocks. Look for places where a series of rocks produces the ideal spot with depth, uniform current, and a place to dart when danger threatens from above.

Logs that stretch across a stream give you the same results. This makes presentation difficult because most small-stream anglers prefer to work upstream, and getting a fly above a log and obtaining a decent drift, if the brush will even let you cast in front of a log, is not fun. But I assure you that more trout will feed above the log—or at its outside point if it does not stretch across the river channel completely— than behind it. Logs that lie along the bank or in midstream parallel to the current are much easier

This submerged log lying parallel to the current offers superb shelter, and because it is right in the main current thread (as seen by the bubbles on the left side), trout can lie right alongside it and feed without being exposed to predators.

to fish and to read—you know trout will be lying alongside the log, and will favor the side of the log closest to the thalweg because that's where the food will be.

Many small creeks, like meadow streams, boggy, lowland streams, or spring creeks, may have few rocks or logs to help you read the water. In these streams, the river channel itself provides most of the clues. Look for a narrowing of the stream channel, which speeds up the water and forms riffles. Riffles provide cover for fish because the distorted surface prevents fish from being seen, and riffles are the food producers in a stream. Where a riffle ends, you'll find a pool, or if not a pool at least a slowing and deepening of the channel. The lip at the downstream end of a riffle provides a perfect place for trout to rest and feed.

Bends in a lowland river will also stimulate a quickening in the current, whether it is manifested in riffles or not. At a bend, on the outside (or concave) part of the stream channel, the faster current is pushed up against the bank and will form deeper undercuts that shelter trout and bring food right to them. As the current lessens below the bend, you will find a shelf that stretches across the stream where the slower current has deposited gravel, silt, or sand. The decrease in depth here acts just like the cushion in front of a rock, and trout will often lie on the boundary between the shallow and deep water, resting comfortably, but ready to dart into the deeper water or undercuts just upstream at the slightest hint of danger.

I live on a small stream that runs through large and productive cornfields in a narrow valley. Over the centuries, the farmers in the valley have

Where this meadow stream makes a bend, a riffle is formed; trout will be concentrated at the lip where the pool begins to deepen, as indicated by the sudden transition to flatter water.

straightened the stream channel so that it doesn't stray into their valuable cropland and instead runs straight against one side of the valley. My property is one of the few places where the stream has been allowed to regain some of its natural meander, and because the stream takes a severe bend in front of my house, it is one of the most productive places on the creek. Just below my house is a long, straight piece of stream that runs for about a half mile before running around another bend. I have tried that straight piece of water again and again, and although a few small pools form where the stream makes a slight bend, it isn't until the next bend that the fishing gets decent. Once I leave my property I'll walk a half mile to fish the next bend instead of wasting my time in the water just downstream of my house.

BEAVER PONDS

Beavers like to create dams and ponds in lowland streams with a low gradient and lots of aspen or other favorite foods close at hand. These create large pools that can hold the largest trout in a stretch of creek because the deeper water and brushy banks offer protection and a slower current where trout can live easy and get fatter. The inlet of a beaver pond is almost always the best place because that's where the most drifting food is concentrated. If you look closely, you can find the channel that represents the old streambed by looking for places devoid of dead trees or brush in the water. Trout will also hang in this deep channel because of the protection and the more constant food supply it provides. Of course the dam itself, at the downstream end of a beaver pond, also provides depth and protection, but I've never found as many trout downstream of beaver dams, in the riffles usually created below them, as one might think. It may be due to the constant movement of brush and silt from the pond above filling in the riffle, or it may be that

the trout below the dam won't tolerate the activity of the beavers. It has just never been as productive a spot for me as the inlet or the middle of a beaver pond.

The one behavior you'll see in beaver ponds that you won't see in many small streams is trout cruising, leaving a specific lie and swimming around looking for food. This is because the current in a beaver pond is often so lethargic that trout can't find enough food along the main current thread, and also because the sluggish flow allows them to move about for food without wasting energy.

Any time a small stream makes a bend, you can count on a nice pool. Generally, the more severe the bend, the deeper the pool.

■ POOLS

Because you sometimes cannot see all the rocks and logs in the water, plus you can't always tell which ones are better than others, it may be better to fish places in a pool rather than looking at specific obstructions on the bottom. A pool in a stream is any piece of water initiated by a riffle or waterfall, followed by a slower, deeper midsection, and ending in a smooth, shallow tail where the current is concentrated. The middle and head of a pool are the easiest places to fish and the ones most people cast to immediately. The middle of the pool has the deepest water, and you already know that depth is important in a shallow stream. The head of the pool has the fastest water, so you can make more mistakes with your casting because a bad cast is veiled by the riffled water and fish have to make a quick decision where the water runs swiftly.

But the tail of a pool, the place most people cast *over* to get to the middle or head, often holds the most and biggest fish in a small pool. It is a trickier place to cast because the water is accelerating and drag often takes over immediately. The water is shallower

than the middle so the fish are often the spookiest ones in the pool, but in the tail the water is smooth, so it's easier to spot drifting food, and the current is narrowed both vertically and horizontally, so fish get more opportunities to feed. Many times fish that hide in the deeper middle of the pool, where food is scarce, drop down into the tail to feed, and where the tail of a pool has big rocks or a log or a shelf for protection, trout may live there all the time. If you pass up the tail you're going to miss some of the best opportunities of the day, and don't worry about the tricky aspects as you'll learn more about countering the problems of the tail in later chapters.

In the middle of the pool, look for that main thread of current and then look for the larger rocks that will provide a good place for a trout to rest and feed. If you can't see the rocks on the bottom because of light conditions or water depth, look for the bump on the surface that betrays the presence of a rock beneath it. Just remember, though, the bump will be about a foot or two downstream of the position of the rock in this shallow water, and trout might be lying in front of the rock. So cast your fly at least two feet above the surface bump.

At the head of a pool, the water in the main current may be too fast for trout, so look along the edges of the fastest water where the surface smoothes out a bit. The seams on either side are almost always the hotspots in a small stream. However, in meadow streams, where the current is slow enough that the center of the main flow is just a gentle riffle rather than a confused torrent, you may find trout right in the main flow as well as along the edges. You should also look for tiny flows off the main current at the head—many times big rocks at the head of a pool concentrate most of the flow down the center or off to one side, but secondary flows of just the right speed might hide small,

The trout in the head of this pool at (1) will be the easiest to catch. Many anglers will spook the two fish feeding in the tail at (2) because they don't approach the pool carefully enough. The fish at (3) will often be missed as well, because even though it is off to the side it is still in a main thread of current.

deep pockets with just the right flow. I know I often focus so much on the main current that I miss these secondary flows until I wade up through the pool to approach the next one, look off to one side, and then mentally kick myself for not taking off the blinders. By that time I've spooked any fish in these hidden pockets, but I try to remember them for the next trip.

▨ POCKET WATER

You'll sometimes find stretches of water in a small stream that offer few distinct pools. The water runs over fields of boulders, but never settles down enough to form a classic pool. This is some of the most exciting water to fish because trout can be almost anywhere, and because the current is uniformly disturbed the fish are easy to approach and you can relax a little without worrying about your every step. You will probably still see a thalweg, but it will often be split up into several threads, or there may be side pockets that offer almost as much depth and flow as the main channel.

In swift pocket water, one of the best ways to locate trout is to look for dark lenses of smooth water between the areas of white foamy water. White water is probably too swift for trout, and the fish have problems seeing food (and your fly!) in the lathered turbulence. A slick, darker surface tells you the water there is slower and deeper than the foam around it, and trout lie in these hidden slots.

In pocket water you can go crazy trying to fish every spot that looks fishy, so you have to look at the whole streambed instead of concentrating on a single rock. Look for places where two current threads join, or where a series of rocks forms a miniature pool, in a deep slot between rocks, or where the stream takes a bend and concentrates flow and depth on one side.

These are likely places for trout in pocket water. Trout (1) is at the tail of a small pocket where current threads converge. Trout (2) and (3) are along the edge of a large boulder and in front of a submerged rock. Trout (4) and (5) are in the deepest pocket in this location. Trout (6) is along the bank, but with the protection of a large rock and still in the main current thread.

Sight Fishing and Hatches on Small Streams

When you fish tiny waters, you don't expect to spot fish in the water, observe dense hatches of aquatic insects, or discover fish rising in every little pocket. It's a game of reading the water, making a careful approach and presentation, and then waiting a breathless few seconds for a slim fish—with all the hues of the stream bottom heightened to maximum vibrancy—to inhale your fly, rising up from its invisible perch beneath the surface. Seeing trout *before* they take your fly is a delicious gift.

If you fish in small streams often enough, you'll sometimes be rewarded with a day where, rather than hunting for spots you think a trout is lying, your pulse will race with the challenge of casting a mayfly imitation over a fish rising every few seconds, or one lying in shallow water feeding on caddis pupae. The richer the stream, the more likely it is that you'll see plentiful hatches of insects. Spring creeks, tailwaters, and meadow streams that run through valleys with rich soil will be the most likely places to encounter a hatch. And if the hatch occurs during low water, you may be able to spy fish in the water. Fish you observe underwater may be rising or eating insects below the surface— or they might be doing both—all of which in the confines of a small stream give you the zenith of fly fishing for trout.

You are more likely to see trout rising in the deepest, longest pools in the evening. Insect hatches generally peak in the evening right at sunset, and the absence of bright sunlight lets trout feel more secure out in the open reaches of a broad pool. On the other hand, you are more likely to enjoy sight-casting with a nymph to subsurface trout in the middle of a bright sunny day, as that's the only time you'll be able to spot them in the water.

Approach trout with extreme caution when they are visible. If you can see them, chances are they can see you, so slow movements and a low profile increase your chances of success. Under normal conditions, when fish are not actively feeding on a hatch, they lie in riffles or alongside cover and the object that protects them may also keep you out of sight. When insects become plentiful, trout move in shallower, more open areas where feeding is easier. Tails of pools, shallow riffles, and side eddies—where the current is slow but not completely stagnant—are places to look.

If it's sunny, look for a trout's shadow, as it is much easier to spot the distinct black line of a shadow than it is to see the camouflaged fish against the stream bottom. Look for movement. A feeding trout sways in the current, and even though you might mistake a strand of aquatic weed for a trout, it's better to be safe than sorry. It also helps to look for parts of a trout and not the entire fish. Chances are you'll spot a fin or tail first, and the tail is often the biggest betrayer of a fish as it waves in the current. "It looks just like a flag waving in the breeze," say my friends Dave and Amelia Jenson, who are uncanny at spotting fish in their Alberta brown trout streams.

If you spot a trout, freeze immediately. One step farther could send the fish bolting for cover. Sometimes you may be too close to make a comfortable cast and it might be necessary to back up; do so by lowering your profile slowly and then retreating back through the same path you used to get there. Don't move from one side to the other, because you already know you approached that fish successfully from the given path. The next step, if you can resist casting right away, is to watch the fish. A trout immobile on the bottom is either scared or asleep—you might try a cast to that fish, but your chances of success are slim. A fish that waves from side to side in the current, or up and down in the water column, is a feeder and is not spooked yet.

If the fish is rising, try to determine the size, shape, and color of the insects it's feeding on. If the fish is not rising but actively feeding under the surface, you may still be able to pick the right nymph if you see some insects hatching. Pick a drab nymph the same size as those insects on the surface—most insect larvae are a dull tan or olive color and a subtle fly is more likely to be taken than a bright one. Small-stream trout are not as suspicious of fly pattern as fish from larger rivers because small streams don't get as much fishing pressure, but selectivity is still hard-wired into every trout, as natural selection chooses those trout that eat safe prey they recognize.

In the thin waters of small streams, you won't get many chances at each fish, so make the first cast count. Make a plan. Look out for currents that might cause drag and make a cast that avoids it. If the sun is off to one side of the fish, make your cast down-sun of the fish so that your line does not cast a shadow over it and the fish sees the fly illuminated and off to its side. It's much more threatening for a fish to see something land on its blind side, and the fish is also more likely to notice the fly on its illuminated side. This is something I learned from the great permit guide Marshall Cutchin, but it is just as true for tiny mountain trout.

Watch the trout's reaction to your first cast. If the fish suddenly dashes for a submerged log you can guess what happened. You're done, move on. If it moves off to one side, your cast probably bothered it slightly but not enough to spook it. A fish that sinks slowly to the bottom has also been alerted that something is not quite right, but has determined that whatever happened when that bug landed on its head was not life-threatening. Don't make another cast if a fish changes its behavior but does not bolt. There's a good chance it will resume feeding in a minute or so. If it does, resist the impulse to begin casting again as soon as it gets into a steady rhythm. Wait until it gets its confidence back, swaying in the current and darting a few inches to grab insects every few seconds.

When Conditions Change

 **Chapter 4** ....

When Conditions Change

Now you have a basic idea of where to find small streams and how to locate trout within them. Bad news—or challenging news—depending on your attitude. Trout streams change dramatically through the course of a year and change moderately with a daily rhythm. Various species sometimes react in unexpected ways to these changes, and even within a small population of isolated trout individuals have personalities. Everything we learn about reading the water and about fishing techniques only gives us guidelines about what to expect. Mother Nature will throw you curves every time out, but that's probably what makes fly fishing so appealing. The good news is that small streams don't change as much as large rivers throughout the day or throughout the season, so with a few guidelines you can fish them in mid-afternoon in April the same way you fish them on an August morning.

Seasonal Changes

■ WINTER

In the southern range of small streams, especially in the Appalachians of Virginia, North Carolina, and Georgia, winter fishing is not much different from late fall and early spring fishing, as long as air temperatures don't stay below freezing for more than two or three days in a row. Water temperatures will be at the minimum for trout activity in the morning, but as sun hits the water or air temperatures rise throughout the day, feeding will begin to pick up. This is the time to fish a weighted nymph or small streamer slowly, close to the bottom, in deeper

PAGES 88–89: Muddy water and bright sunlight combine to make fly fishing very challenging.

OPPOSITE: The smaller the stream, the less likely it is to find seasonal and daily changes.

pools, but if the water is low and clear trout may even rise to a dry fly in January in the Smokies. Small-stream trout are always on the lookout for a meal, and just because you don't see any aquatic insects on the water and all the terrestrial insects are fast asleep until spring, don't rule out a dry fly. Food is food, and if a trout is hungry enough, it can see its intended prey, and it's not too much effort to rise a foot off the bottom to eat it, a dry fly might work just fine. Trout don't read the fishing magazines that tell you dry flies don't work in winter.

But in most small streams, where anchor ice pushes fish into deep pools and water temperatures are so low that the fish eat sparingly, winter is a time to tie flies and plan your spring trips. Small streams in the Sierras or the Rockies might not even be accessible without a long hike on snowshoes, and in many states trout season is closed during the winter. That doesn't mean you can't do some scouting though. If you live close to a pocket of small streams, or if you're on a ski vacation and want to get your trout-fishing fix for a few hours, take a hike along a stream you suspect may hold trout. Scouting in winter can give you some tips on where to fish when you come back during a warmer season.

First, look for anchor ice that completely chokes a stream. Ice that forms all the way to the bottom will either push fish downstream into deeper, ice-free pools or it may kill them outright. Where you see extensive anchor ice, fishing won't be productive in early spring—but it might be later in the summer when fish move upstream as water temperatures in the lower elevations get too warm to hold sufficient dissolved oxygen. On the other hand, if nighttime temperatures have fallen below zero degrees Fahrenheit for three days in a row and you find a small stream free of anchor ice, you can assume the fish in that place will be happy and healthy come spring.

Look for winter trout in the deeper, slower pools.

I find some of my best small-stream spots driving to work on subzero mornings. I look for streams free of anchor ice, but I also look for pockets of steam rising from small stretches of a creek. Steam (it's actually ice clouds) rising from a stream means that spot is much warmer than the air, and invariably indicates springs coming into the stream from a hidden source. A mile from my house is one stretch that always steams on cold mornings, and I find that the pools downstream of the spot fish better in early spring and in the heat of summer, because the spring flow keeps the water warmer in early spring and colder in August.

▓ SPRING

Small streams are always closer to a source of groundwater than bigger rivers, and because they drain smaller floodplains they don't get as high and dirty in early spring. In Vermont, when the Battenkill is high, cold, and dirty in late April as the snow begins to melt, I can find low, clear water in Stream No. 3 (I told you I wasn't going to kiss-and-tell in this book), and if I drive upstream to the headwaters of the XYZ River, I can find the same thing. This doesn't mean the fishing is always terrific—it might still be too cold for active feeding even in the headwaters and you might be lucky to catch one little fish. But at least I know the fish can see my fly and if I can put it right in front of their noses I might get a trout to move for it. In a filthy, roiling river I can't even be sure of that!

At exactly what temperature trout begin to feed actively varies with the species of trout and even among local populations. Brook and cutthroat trout in headwater streams don't experience much variation in temperature throughout the season, so they may be as eager to feed in April as they are in June because they have adapted to feeding in colder temperatures. In my experience, rainbow trout have a wide temperature tolerance, greater than any other species of trout, so they may also feed actively in cold water if they are adapted to it. Local populations of rainbow trout have been observed feeding at as low as 36 degrees and as high as 80 degrees. Brown trout don't seem to be as adaptable to wide swings in temperature. If you're fishing a small stream you know is full of brown trout and the water temperature is below 45 degrees, it may seem like the creek is completely lifeless. Come back in a few weeks and you might catch fish in every little pocket.

Mountain streams fed by snow or glacier runoff can exhibit what seems like a backward yield in fishing success. On cold days, the water stays low and clear, but on warm, sunny days snow and ice begin to melt and creek levels rise, the water gets dirty, and water temperatures sometimes get even colder as the day progresses. So contrary to what we've been taught about early spring fishing, your best luck might come before noon when the air is still chilly. In my experience, given the choice between cold, clear water with low flows and higher, dirtier water, I'll take the cold, clear conditions any time on small streams.

Small-stream trout spend the winter in deeper, slower pools where they are protected from anchor ice and where they can maintain a low rate of metabolism in the cold water without working hard to fight the current. Fish will remain in the deeper overwintering pools until mid-spring, when water temperatures rise above 50 degrees and the fish can survive in the food-rich riffles, so continue to look for them in deep, slow water until then. Look for places where the stream slope plateaus and stay away from places with long, uninterrupted expanses of fast water. Beaver ponds by nature are slow and deep and are perhaps the best place to try in early spring when you know it's really too early for good fishing but you just can't stand being away from the water.

Once the water temperature in a small stream hits 50 degrees, you're in the glory days. Fish begin to feed actively, and dries, wets, nymphs, and streamers will all interest trout. As water gets above 55 degrees, fish will move several feet for a fly if

In the high water of spring, trout may still be concentrated in the deeper pools until the water temperatures go above 50 degrees.

they're not frightened and the fly is reasonably close. This is the very best time to explore small streams to prove their worth. If the water temperature is 55 degrees and you see no fish rising and none even splash at your flies, you can assume that the stream holds few trout—or that someone around the bend just waded through the water and frightened all of them.

At this magic time it is rare to find a stream that does not host a heavy emergence of aquatic insects at dusk. It varies with latitude, but if you examine one of the larger pools on a small stream in mid-May in the southern Appalachians, June in the Northeast or Midwest, or early July in the high-mountain regions of the West and don't see fish rising, keep poking around until you find a stream or a stretch of stream where the fish are rising. It can be tough to fish a small stream at dark, but now you know where the fish live and because small-stream trout are more likely to feed throughout the day than fish in bigger rivers, you can come back when you can see your fly and your backcast and expect to be rewarded.

■ SUMMER

One of the most pleasant and rewarding aspects of small-stream fishing is that the glory days of spring are extended through the summer. If you get far enough upstream you'll never experience the dog days of August in small streams, because water temperatures stay in the prime 55- to 65-degree range all summer long. With their narrow and usually shaded stream channels and their proximity to groundwater that reflects the annual mean temperature of their latitude, most small streams stay cold enough to keep trout actively feeding, even in the middle of the day in July and August. The food supply of most small-stream trout is primarily terrestrial and not aquatic insects, and the peak of terrestrial insect populations is during the heat of summer. So when larger rivers are filled with boats and their wide pools are baked by the sun, raising water temperatures and lowering dissolved oxygen, small streams are at their peak.

Water temperatures during summer in small streams in northern latitudes are seldom a problem unless a stream is far from its source; in fact, many small streams in New England, northern Michigan and Minnesota, and in the high mountains of the Rockies and Sierras don't hit that prime water temperature of 60 degrees until the height of summer. However, streams at lower altitudes, especially those in the mountains of the Southeast below 2,000 feet, will get too warm for active trout feeding, possibly reaching the lethal limit for trout survival, so the fish begin to move upstream in search of colder water. Under these conditions you should either quit fishing or move up in altitude.

Small streams in headwater areas may get an influx of fish, often larger fish than they support at other times of the year, during the summer. Brook trout that live at lower altitudes will move upstream in the summer to find cooler water temperatures with higher dissolved oxygen. These migrants, often bigger than the resident fish, join the brook trout already living in the headwaters. Rainbow trout are an especially footloose species and even small-stream fish will move for many miles upstream in summer, acting just like miniature steelhead. Cutthroats move around as well, although not to the same degree as rainbows. Brown trout will move if conditions get severe, but this species is a lot more likely to stay put and not move upstream to find cooler water. Brown trout, in fact—although they are much more tolerant of warm temperatures than brook trout—may even put themselves at risk during hot droughts given their predilection to stay put.

The small stream on my property has wild brook, brown, and rainbow trout in its pools during the spring and early summer when water temperatures are prime. It's not a headwater stream, but it is midway between the headwaters and the point where water temperatures get too warm for trout during the summer, so it's an excellent place to observe this movement. In early spring I see and catch brook trout, but by July they disappear. I imagine they move up into even smaller tributaries and the stream's headwaters, where water temperatures stay cold all summer. If we have a hot, dry summer, one day I'll walk down to the river and find the pools filled with rainbows, far more than I usually see in spring. Sometimes these migrants stay put, and if the summer is really hot they'll continue to move upstream. The brown trout, however, are always in the same spots. I see no influx of browns until they begin to move upstream to spawn in November, and the same fish are in the same spot, week after week. I've discovered this because I can see how many fish are living in some of the pools, and because I fin clip some fish to mark them.

High-altitude streams will not reach their prime until the height of summer because it's the only time water temperatures go above 50 degrees.

▪ FALL

Popular wisdom holds that fall, with its lowering water temperatures, stimulates trout feeding. This is the case in southern small streams, where temperatures in many of the creeks at lower elevations approach a lethal limit for trout, and the fish move upstream or tuck into deep pools and spring seeps to ride out the warm weather. Fall in the Smokies or the Blue Ridge Mountains is a time to renew relationships with small streams at all altitudes, not just the headwater streams tucked high into the mountains.

However, in northern streams, small-stream trout fishing hits a wall about the time the leaves fall from the trees and the cold rains of autumn begin. It isn't just water temperature that puts a damper on fishing. Growth rate studies of small-stream trout show that feeding slows down beginning in late summer. I've never seen any strong evidence why. It's true that brook and brown trout are fall spawners and they may begin to concentrate more on spawning behavior than on fattening up. But rainbows and cutthroats, both spring spawning species, also seem to slow down in the fall. It's not that you won't catch trout in the fall, you just won't catch as many. Pools that would give up four or five little trout in midsummer might draw one half-hearted rise in October.

The one tip I have for fishing in the fall in northern streams is to move the fly slightly, whether you are fishing a dry, nymph, or streamer. I believe with all the leaves and other debris falling into small streams that fish get turned off to surface food and food that just falls into the water without any appearance of life. It doesn't take a trout many bites of small leaves and twigs before they begin to look for a glimmer of life before they inhale their food. You don't have the same issue in southern streams. Trees lose their leaves due to cues from photoperiod, not temperature, and deciduous leaves begin to fall in North Carolina at about the same time as they do in Michigan. However, the difference in the southern states is that insects are still active because the air temperature is warmer, so when leaves fall off the trees they bring a bonanza of ants, beetles, leafhoppers, and caterpillars along with them.

Fall leaves can make small-stream fishing difficult and, due to all the debris on the water, it's often necessary to twitch the fly to catch a trout's attention.

Daily and Other Short-Term Changes

■ TEMPERATURE

In a typical trout stream in midsummer, water temperature makes the rules. For example, in early morning water temperatures are low, and they rise through the morning as the air temperature rises and sunlight warms the water. This often creates a strong feeding period in mid-morning because trout react strongly to these changes, plus aquatic insects also hatch in response to a rise in temperature. Around noon, water temperatures get warm enough to slow down both trout and insect activity; strong sunlight increases the chance that aquatic insects will get eaten by swallows and flycatchers; and trout are under increased risk of detection by mergansers, herons, ospreys, and otters. In the

evening, insects begin hatching after sunlight leaves the water and trout respond to them. Water temperatures are still at a maximum for the day even after the sun goes down, but the presence of aquatic insects and the absence of predators puts trout on the feed again. You'll find this daily fluctuation more at lower altitude, lower gradient small streams.

Small streams at higher altitudes or closer to a source of a spring don't have the same range of daily temperature fluctuations. Water temperatures are more constant over a 24-hour period, but air temper-

fishing does not have the "down times" that you see on famous trout rivers. The trout are always eager to feed—*especially* in the middle of the day.

■ FLOODS

There is nothing more frustrating to a fly fisher than high water. It discourages trout from feeding on the surface, it is difficult to get your fly down to fish at the bottom of deep pools, and if the water is dirty it only magnifies the inability of a trout to find your fly. Luckily, small streams flood less often than big rivers and their floods are often discouraging but not a total catastrophe. Small streams don't always get dirty when their waters rise, so at most you have to deal with several inches to perhaps two feet of additional water in the stream channel, plus an increased current flow. In fact, when torrential rains flood popular trout streams, smart anglers head for tributaries and headwater streams even if they don't particularly care for small-stream fishing. Even to those who only look for big trout, small trout are better than none at all.

This difference means that, at most, you might have to tie on a nymph with a tungsten bead at its head or add a couple of split shot to your leader instead of walking away from the water shaking your head in disgust. In big rivers, high water usually means the end of dry-fly fishing because a trout that was lying in two feet of water, where it was an easy slide to the surface to pluck a bug from the film, might suddenly be covered by four additional feet of turbid flow. In a small stream, a few extra inches of water will still allow trout to see your dry fly, although you may have to find quieter pockets of water off to the side of the main flow. This is the time to fish a big size 8 or 10 dry fly. Trout in the small stream you are fishing may never see a large stonefly like a golden

atures do fluctuate so that terrestrial insects, the primary food of small-stream trout, are more abundant in the middle of the day. Trout in small streams can and do respond to aquatic insect hatches, but this daily fluctuation of hatches is less pronounced in small streams. The bottom line is that small-stream trout

tional terrestrial food like worms into a stream and high water often stimulates aquatic insect hatches.

So in high flows, imagine where trout would be lying at normal flows, and try to imagine what the brook looked like before the flood. If a small stream is a foot higher than normal, pockets that look great right now might have been almost dry a few days ago, and chances are trout have not moved into them, but stayed in the same places they were at low water. It's more difficult to get a trout to rise to a dry in high flows and it is harder to get a nymph down to its level, but by fishing in these tougher places at least you will be placing your fly where a trout may be living.

DROUGHTS

Droughts scare me because of their long-term effect on the health of small streams. They expose more fish to predators because as a stream channel shrinks there are fewer places for a trout to hide. A drought in the spring or fall spawning season can affect the spawning success of fish. Some small streams literally disappear if the water table gets too low. But I have to confess to you, fly fishing small streams during a drought can be superb, especially dry-fly fishing.

During a drought (or during normal low-water periods, for that matter), there will be little doubt where the fish are. They'll be in the deepest water in each pool, right under the main current flow. Watch the bubble line as it progresses through a pool and always place your fly along that narrow

stone or a giant mayfly like a green drake, but they will rise to one if it looks remotely like food.

It's important to determine if a stream is higher than normal because it prevents you from fishing places that might be barren of fish. The best indicator is foliage along the edges of the stream. Once spring plants begin to grow in the early season, certain types will thrive right at the edge of the water and will continue to grow there throughout the season. Few will grow underwater, so if you see a patch of wild mint or young willow shoots with stems underwater, you can immediately tell the creek is in flood, and you can even tell how much higher than normal by the amount of stem underwater.

A trout chooses a place in a stream that protects it from current even at lower flows, and when the water rises from a rainstorm, the place that the fish has chosen doesn't get much faster. The water on the surface moves at a much faster pace than at normal flows, but the flow close to the bottom and near obstructions stays about the same because of the friction between objects and the flow. What a rise in water does is place an extra layer of velocity and depth between your offering and the fish, but a fish is quite content to ride it out in the same place, perhaps even more content, because floods wash addi-

In drought conditions, it will be easy to tell where the trout live, but they will be tough to approach without scaring them.

lane. While you might have to cast your fly into a half dozen little pockets to catch trout under normal flows, it will be patently obvious where they'll be in low water. If any trout live in the pool, you know you'll be placing your fly right on target.

Droughts reduce the overall depth and current flow in a small stream so trout will be ultra-spooky. You will need to exercise more caution in approaching a pool (you may spook all the trout regardless under these conditions), and you may have to use a finer leader and a smaller fly than normal. In fact, when fishing low, summer water conditions, it's often a good idea to make a cast well away from a pool. You may have to fish a pool from the pool downstream of it, and you may also find the need to throw your line over 10 feet of dry land to get five feet of drift through a still,

shallow pool. This is often a case of only one good cast in each pool, so plan your approach carefully and make that first cast count. It will be the best chance you have to pluck a trout from a pool the size of a small bathtub.

Dry-fly fishing under drought conditions is the best approach. The water may be so shallow that fish can't even see subsurface food because there will be minimal flow above their heads to search for prey, as trout can see a piece of food drifting on the surface from much farther away than they can something drifting below the surface. Aquatic insects don't hatch as regularly in low water, either. So the bulk of their food will be from terrestrial insects falling into the water and drifting in the surface film, and the trout will be primed to grab anything on the surface that looks remotely edible.

When Big Trout Inhabit Small Streams

Few anglers poke around in small streams looking for big trout, but occasionally a brook you can straddle will give up a trout that doesn't even seem like it has room to turn around. A 16-inch trout from a tiny pool gives more thrills than it would in a river, and if the stream is brushy the chances of landing a trophy are slim. But catching a trout you have to chase through three or four pools to land is the stuff of daydreams for years to come.

Here are some places you might find trout weighing more than one pound in tiny waters:

■ A stream that hosts large migrations of mice or has seasonal plagues of grasshoppers. Trout are capable of maximizing their energy intake for short periods of time once a year and growing quite quickly if the food they capture is large and high in calories.

■ A tiny watershed that produces hatches of big aquatic insects like green drakes or hex mayflies, or salmonfly or skwala stoneflies. Again, even though the large and abundant food source is available to trout for only a few weeks, they make good use of it.

■ A stream that runs into a much larger river known to produce big trout. Large trout may enter small streams to spawn for a month or so each year, and if there are no dams to prevent access to the headwaters, trout will migrate many miles to return to the gravel beds where they hatched from eggs years ago. During midsummer, trout will also migrate into small streams when water temperatures in the bigger river go above 70 degrees. Small streams, closer to the source of springs, are colder than wide rivers in the summer.

■ A brook that runs into or out of a lake or pond. Few trout can spawn successfully in still water, so to reproduce they must enter running waters for at least a few weeks every year. In addition, lake-dwelling baitfish like smelt enter moving water to spawn in the spring and will ascend even tiny brooks.

■ A stream that supports a dense population of baitfish like sculpins. Typically small streams don't harbor large populations of baitfish, but sometimes low-gradient meadow streams have surprisingly high populations of sculpins.

■ Spring creeks, especially those with dense beds of rooted aquatic vegetation. The plants harbor large populations of crustaceans like scuds and sow bugs, and these high-fat, high-protein food sources are available to trout year-round, so trout grow quickly.

If you are looking for large migratory trout in small streams, it pays to know what species live in the lake or big river into which a small trout enters. Brown and brook trout are fall spawners and will enter small streams any time from late August to November. Rainbows spawn from February through May, although some hatchery strains of rainbows are said to spawn in the fall as well. Cutthroats spawn in the spring and the exact time is determined mostly by altitude, as those at lower elevations spawn in February through May, while those at high altitudes like Yellowstone National Park may not complete spawning until July.

If you suspect you are fishing a brook that contains spawning trout, the standard dry and nymph patterns might be ignored by these comparative giants. Trout on a spawning migration are aggressive, even though they do little feeding, and males in particular will attack smaller trout or baitfish. Streamers are most effective for all species, and rainbows and cutthroats also seem to be fond of eating eggs that roll out of the gravel nest made by the female (it's not cannibalism as eggs that don't get deposited beneath the gravel are wasted anyway), so bright pink and orange flies are also deadly. Once brook and brown trout are finished spawning in late fall and begin to drop back down into larger rivers, water temperatures are so low they don't feed much and are difficult to catch. But when rainbows and cutthroats finish spawning in the spring the waters are gradually warming to an optimum level so the fish may feed heavily on aquatic insects to regain the body weight they lost during spawning and fighting.

Outside of spawning migrations, small streams with an abundant food supply can harbor large resident trout that stay in the same pool throughout the year. Brown trout in particular will take up residence in the deepest pool with the most overhead cover. They can live their entire lives here unmolested and unseen by anglers because they stay hidden under cover most of the time, venturing out only at night or under the cover of dirty water from a sudden rainstorm.

Ten years ago I bought a house on a small stream filled with small wild brown and rainbow trout. One pool in my backyard was much deeper than the others and was bordered by a jumble of submerged logs. Even though I fished there several times a week, hunted ducks along its banks, and walked the dog twice a day right next to the pool, for the first few years I lived there I never saw a trout more than 12 inches long—never even spooked one, much less saw one feeding—until a state fisheries crew with electro-shocking gear ran a pair of probes into the pool and came up with a brown trout more than 20 inches long.

Fishing in a stream barely 10 feet wide at night is not an easy task, and I really didn't want to catch that fish at night so I never tried. Two years went by and after another electro-shocking session, another huge trout came out of the same pool. Whether it was the same fish I'm not sure, but that pool was obviously a fine place for a brown trout to live out its years unmolested. Two more years went by, and one spring evening I walked down to the river after dinner with my wife, son, and dog, and took a rod with a single streamer tied to the leader. The river was high and dirty from a recent rainstorm, and on my second cast I finally caught that fish—or its twin sister.

So if your favorite small stream has a deep, brushy pool where nothing ever touches your dry fly or nymph, it may be inhabited by a single large brown trout that either scares the smaller fish away or eats them. Try that pool some evening or early morning just after a rainstorm. Just make sure your tippet is at least 2X.

ORVIS
ROD AND TACKLE

Hy-Flote
Dust

ORV
ROD AND
SUPER
TIPPET

 **Chapter 5** ....

Fly Selection and Special Tackle for Small Streams

Fly Selection in Small Streams

Even though mounds of books on aquatic entomology and matching the hatch precisely dominate the shelves in bookstores and fly shops, every scientific study on the feeding habits of trout has shown that they are not only opportunistic feeders, but they most often select the largest prey species available. The reason I think fly fishers get sidetracked is that they've all seen the times when trout seem to prefer tiny olive mayflies while the bigger green drakes drift downstream among the smaller flies, seemingly unmolested. But trout also select prey they are familiar with and are easiest to capture. The time when they ignore bigger flies to eat smaller stuff is probably when the tiny helpless flies are easier to capture than the big fluttering duns, and perhaps when the bigger flies are just beginning to hatch for the season and trout have not gotten wise to them yet.

Small-stream trout, because they don't see as much food drifting past, are even more opportunistic than fish in larger rivers, and because between 50 and 90 percent of their diet includes large terrestrial insects that widely vary in shape and color, they are less selective than fish in big rivers, which see daily emergences of the same aquatic insects for weeks at a time. Stomach content analysis of small-stream trout shows that they prefer the big stuff—big beetles, big moths, and big ants. This makes fly selection on small streams easy.

PAGES 106–107: It doesn't take much gear to fish small streams. A small box of flies, a pair of forceps for debarbing and removing flies from fish, a couple of spools of tippet material, and a pair of snips should be enough. If you fish dry flies, it helps to have a gel-style floatant to pre-treat your flies and a white dessicant powder to keep them floating high after they get drowned. Carry it all in a couple of pockets or in a small pack or bag.

OPPOSITE: There's no need to agonize over fly selection in small streams. The fish aren't usually very picky.

DRY FLIES

Scratch a small-stream angler and you'll find someone who loves to fish dry flies—with good reason. Except for occasional high-water periods and from late fall until spring, when water temperatures are below 45 degrees, dry flies are the easiest and most effective flies to use in small streams. In the hands of a skilled small-stream fanatic, they are as effective as worms. Fish in shallow water can always see a dry fly; they don't have to battle the current to get at a floating fly that is only a foot or two above their position; they can see dry flies from farther away than they can a sunken fly; and they are conditioned to eating terrestrial insects that fall into the water and drift downstream.

Because small-stream fish are opportunistic to a fault, your fly selection can be minimal. In fact, most small-stream anglers I talk to use only three or four different dry flies, and if pushed into a corner most will admit they can get by with just a Parachute Adams in sizes 10 through 18. Of course, that takes too much of the fun out of the experience, and I have had times when I was glad I had a choice of patterns, but the Parachute Adams is absolutely a don't-leave-home-without-it pattern.

If no one has recommended specific fly patterns to you, what should you look for? The number one standard is visibility. Small-stream trout fishing requires precise casting, and even wilderness fish are extremely sensitive to drag, that unnatural motion of a fly pulled contrary to the flow of the current because it is attached to a leader and line. If you don't know where your fly is drifting, you won't know if it's floating over the right spot and you won't be able to tell if it's dragging. Yes, you might also miss strikes, although this is not as critical as you might think, because most small-stream trout take a dry fly eagerly and there won't be much of a question of a take—if you can't see your fly and you see a splash anywhere near where your fly could be floating, tighten the line. As long as you don't rip your line off the water you'll either just slide the line through the pool or hook a fish.

In small streams you often fish more tumbling, turbulent water than on bigger rivers, and in many of them you fish beneath a shaded canopy, so the fly is even more difficult to spot. The fly doesn't have to float high as long as something sticks up above the water for you to track. In fact, because terrestrial insects ride lower in the water than aquatic insects, a fly that rides low in the water, but is still highly visible, is the best of both worlds.

Flies that fall into this category include, of course, the Parachute Adams, or any other fly with

Greenback cutthroats taught me the value of having a few small hatch-matching flies in my small-stream box.

parachute wings or upright and divided hair wings, like a Royal Wulff. Elk or deer hair wings in a light shade are also highly visible, and it's no accident that the Elk Hair Caddis and the Stimulator are among the most popular small-stream dry flies in the world. Of course, the bigger the fly, the more visible it is, and I will often start with a size 10 Stimulator, with its large elk hair wing, when most people are fishing a size 14 Parachute Adams.

You see all kinds of dry flies with pink and orange wings made from synthetic materials, because at first glance they seem to be more visible. I can't argue that in foamy water they're not easy to pick out in contrast to the white foam. However, I still feel a pure white wing is the best for visibility, especially in the low light of evenings or on cloudy days. A bright white wing reflects all colors so it is more likely to pick up any available light. I've also seen parachute flies tied with black wings because they are supposed to show up better with heavy glare on the water. Maybe this is true in theory, but when you are fishing small streams you move from one water type and one light condition to another quickly, and I know white wings are more visible under most light conditions.

Knowing that small-stream fish eat a lot of terrestrial insects, there is a tendency to fill your fly box with ant, beetle, and grasshopper imitations. These flies will work just fine, but I don't think you have to worry about imitating terrestrials with specific imitations. An Elk Hair Caddis does a fine job of imitating moths and small grasshoppers, as well as the caddis flies it was designed to imitate. You might not think a Humpy looks much like a beetle because of its upright wings and long tail, but beetles fly quite well, and when a beetle falls into the water it doesn't always have the clean outline of the beetles you see crawling around your rose bushes. Sometimes they land while still flying, so the wings are spread out and the legs are wiggling, and a bushy Humpy might be a great imitation of the naturals. At first glance a Royal Wulff looks nothing like an ant, with its red floss middle surrounded by green peacock herl. But once a Royal Wulff gets wet, the floss and the peacock herl darken and suddenly you have a fly with a body that looks pretty close to an ant. Because small-stream trout pick

It's always safe insurance to have a few hatch-matching flies appropriate to the season, including mayfly duns, spinners, emergers, and small terrestrial insects.

at different kinds of insects all day long, both aquatic and terrestrial bugs, picking a fly that suggests many different kinds of prey in an impressionistic way, but nothing in particular, is probably the safest route.

I do like to keep a few smaller, more precise imitations of insects in my fly box just in case. I learned this lesson the hard way on a small cutthroat stream in the Colorado Rockies. To get to the stream we had a vertical climb of 2,000 feet and it was a warm day, so instead of my usual fishing vest loaded with fly boxes I just stuck a single fly box filled with dry flies, nothing smaller than a size 16, into my pocket. I'd never met a small-stream trout that wouldn't take a Parachute Adams—until then. I asked Tim Romano and Kirk Deeter, the locals who were showing me their secret stream, what they usually fished and Tim mentioned small ants and beetles, size 18. Hah! I'd show these guys what a big dry fly could do.

I was humbled. We separated, each of us taking a stretch of creek. I didn't catch many fish, and the few that came to my fly made halfhearted splashes that seldom connected. Walking along the bank I noticed tiny black ants all over the ground. Then I saw a few size 20 blue-wing olive mayflies hatching. At one point I settled into a small pool where I could see a half dozen cutthroats feeding steadily on and just below the surface, and I spent the next 45 minutes watching in fascination as the fish tipped up to my bigger dry flies, only to settle back to the bottom without taking my offering. I went through every fly in my box, but the fish were having no part of my big dries. I would have killed for a size 20 Parachute Olive, size 18 Pheasant Tail nymph, or a size 16 Black Ant. But these were all 2,000 feet below in the car and I was too proud to ask Tim or Kirk for a fly.

I came away with a new respect for cutthroats, supposedly the "dumbest" of the trout species, and a vow never to fish a small stream without a few small ants and olive mayfly imitations in my box. This is not a common scenario on small streams—typically the fish are pushovers—but when fishing unfamiliar streams you never know what you might find and it's a shame to be so far from home with a fly box that's not up to the task. So do a little investigating and find out what hatches are common that time of year. You probably won't find any information on hatches in tiny streams, so look for the nearest larger trout stream that does publish hatch charts in books or on the Internet. For instance, never fish west of the Mississippi during the summer without a few dries that imitate the Pale Morning dun mayfly and size 10 Golden Stones. Never fish in the East without some Pale Evening dun or Rusty Spinner imitations. You may never need these, but if you do find yourself faced with unusually picky fish you will be glad you have them.

Carrying popular nymphs in different weights is more important than carrying lots of patterns. The top Pheasant Tail nymph is unweighted for shallow runs. The middle one is tied with a brass bead for slightly deeper water. The one at the bottom is made with a large tungsten bead to scrape the bottom in deep pools and fast water.

NYMPHS AND WET FLIES

In my experience dry flies are effective about 90 percent of the time on small streams, and dries are easier and more fun to use because everything is visual. But on occasion, usually when water temperatures are below 50 degrees or the water is higher than normal, you may have better success with a wet fly or nymph. A wet fly can also be more effective than a dry on low-gradient, lowland streams; one of the favorite techniques of anglers in the Driftless Region of the Midwest is to swing a soft-hackled wet fly through shallow riffles. In this thin water, casting a wet fly well above a trout's position and letting it swing down to the fish disturbs the water less than casting a dry fly right over its head, and it's much easier to fish a wet fly than a dry fly downstream because drag on the fly does not put the fish off on a subsurface presentation.

Because trout in small streams are more opportunistic in their feeding habits than fish in bigger rivers, you don't need many different patterns. I feel it's more important to carry a couple of patterns in a variety of sizes and sink rates than it is to have a dozen different fly patterns in the same size. It's hard to prove this, but I don't think I've ever met a small-stream trout that would refuse a Prince nymph and would only eat a Hare's Ear.

Pick one bulky nymph like a Hare's Ear to imitate big stoneflies, caddis pupae, and large flattened mayflies with large gills. Then add a slimmer nymph, I suggest a Pheasant Tail, to match smaller mayflies and stoneflies. The most important consideration is to carry these in size 8 through 18, and in various sink rates. In other words, fill your box with unweighted Hare's Ear nymphs for shallow riffles, regular beadhead versions for slightly deeper water, and a few with tungsten heads for scratching bottom in the deep, dark plunge pools. With these flies you should be able to fish your nymph at all depths without the need to carry split shot to get the fly deeper. To these nymphs I'd add a few soft-hackle wet flies in sizes 12 through 16 for fishing downstream on a swing. I am not sure why soft-hackle wets work better on a swing than weighted nymphs, but from my experience, and from everyone else I've talked to, they sure seem to, especially in shallow water.

STREAMERS

Small streams don't have the dense populations of baitfish that larger rivers do, and the farther upstream you go in a first-order stream the fewer baitfish you'll find, until at the very headwaters the only fish you'll find living there are trout. So small-stream trout don't eat as many baitfish, and a fly as big as some of the streamers used today might scare every trout in a little headwater brook. Still, a small streamer fly in size 10 or 12 can imitate a crayfish or large stonefly, and in the lower reaches of small streams you'll find these creatures, as well as a larger population of sculpins, dace, and other minnows. A streamer can also elicit a territorial response from trout, so a fish may nip at a streamer thinking that it's an intruder in its space.

Especially in high water, a streamer might be large enough for a trout to notice when smaller nymphs and dry flies are hard to see. I was fishing a small stream in the foothills of the Blue Ridge Mountains of Virginia one dreary November day with a few friends. The water was about a foot above normal and the brook and rainbow trout weren't coming to the surface for our dry flies as I'd been told they usually did, and nymphs weren't doing any better. I sat down on the bank to watch my friend Rick Wagner work upstream through a couple of pools and saw him take four trout in a row on a size 14 Conehead Muddler, fishing it upstream almost dead drift with an occasional twitch as opposed to the standard way most of us fish streamers, retrieving the fly with constant strips.

Although I still don't fish streamers often on small streams, they can save the day when fish ignore everything else. As with nymphs, you don't need to carry many patterns. A bright fly like a Mickey Finn plus a bulkier, drab-colored sculpin or Woolly

Bugger in size 12 is probably all you'll need, but as with nymphs, try to take both weighted and unweighted versions. An unweighted Woolly Bugger is fine for shallow pools and riffles, but when faced with a deep plunge pool at the base of a waterfall you will need a streamer that gets below the surface currents fast, and nothing does this like a streamer with a tungsten bead or cone at its head. If you're caught without a weighted streamer, you can also pinch a split shot on the leader right at the head of the fly.

Choosing Equipment for Small Streams

▨ ROD LENGTH

Because small-stream trout are usually tiny, many anglers feel they need a short rod to match the size of the trout. You don't always need a super-short fly rod to fish small streams. In fact, a rod shorter than seven feet can be a hindrance, especially when fishing pocket water where drag is tricky. The longer the rod, the easier it is to keep line off the water, and the less line on the water, the less likely it is that conflicting currents will take control of your fly and pull it in a direction that conflicts with the way natural objects drift. On the other hand, if the streams you fish are tight and brushy, a rod that is too long will catch on branches when you want to make a cast, and might prevent you from setting the hook.

Rods shorter than seven feet are for tiny, brushy streams where no other rod will work. You do have a foot more of working room with a six-and-a-half-foot rod than you do with a seven-and-a-half-foot rod, and that working room is not just behind you, but over your head and in front of you. However, before you buy that six-and-a-half-foot rod, make sure you really need it. Most small-stream fishing is done by working upstream, and often you have enough clearance behind you to get away with a rod up to eight feet long, as long as the canopy does not extend across the top of the stream.

For a wide variety of small streams, the best length is between seven and eight feet. Rods in this range let you cast in pretty tight spots, yet still have enough reach to keep line off the water as needed. The all-important roll cast is also more difficult with a shorter rod. Rods between eight and eight-and-a-half feet long are fine for mountain streams with wide rocky banks and sparse brush or for meadow streams with low brush, where you want to keep your backcast higher. Rods nine feet and longer will work on small streams as long as you have plenty of backcast room, but they are overkill for small-stream fishing, where you don't need long casts or the ability to mend line 40 feet in front of you. Still, if all you have is a nine-foot rod, use it! I'll give you some casting tricks in the next chapter that will help.

▨ FLY LINES

As with rod length, there is a tendency to buy a small-stream rod that calls for a light fly line. The fish are small, right? Yes, but the flies aren't. Although it's rare to fish a giant size 4 Foam Hopper or a size 2 Zonker in small streams, the most common fly sizes are between size 10 and 16. It's difficult to push a size 10 dry fly with a 2-weight or 3-weight line, and even though the temptation to use a tiny, lightweight rod on small streams is strong because it makes the fish feel bigger, these lighter line sizes can make casting more difficult, even though most casts are 30 feet or less. A 4-weight or 5-weight rod makes more sense for these fly sizes, balancing the ability to push a bigger dry fly or nymph with enough delicacy to make stealthy casts over spooky fish. A 6-weight is probably too heavy for most small streams, as in clear,

OPPOSITE: A longer rod helps hold more line off the water in tricky places like the tails of pools.

shallow water it will land with enough disturbance to scare some trout.

Matching a fly line with a rod gets a little trickier than buying a rod off the rack and picking the line size the manufacturer tells you to use. Most fly rod line size ratings are made so the rod casts optimally at around 40 feet, and in most small streams a cast that long might be around the next bend. This is not always the case, as some rods, like the Orvis Superfine Series, are made for small-stream work and their optimum casting distance with the rated fly line is about 20 feet. When buying a small-stream rod, unless you know it was made for small streams, it's best to try the rod with the rated line size plus one line size heavier. If the rod was made for longer casts, the heavier line will bring out its action at shorter distances and may be perfect. Or, if you already own a rod that you use for bigger rivers, you might want to invest in a second line that is one size heavier just for small-stream fishing.

It's often stated that slow-action fly rods are better for small-stream fishing because they load better at short distances. It's true that most slow (or full-flex) rods load well with 20 feet of line, but it's more a matter of the load on the rod than it is its action. This gets confusing because no two people agree on how to describe fly-rod action, but to simplify it, consider that action refers to the way a rod bends under a given load of fly line. A fast-action (or tip-flex) rod bends more at the tip than into the middle and butt of the rod, and you can make a fast-action rod cast well on short casts by increasing the line size you put on it. Most fly fishers think a fast-action rod is stiffer because most rod companies rate the line size on their fast or tip-flex rods so that they cast better beyond 40 feet. But increasing the load on a typical fast-action rod by using one or even two line sizes heavier can make it a superb small-stream rod.

In small-stream fishing, the only fly line you'll need is a floater.

Tight spots call for a short rod, one under seven feet long.

In mountain streams with a wide floodplain, a short rod is seldom needed as there is plenty of room in the middle of the stream.

Flies hung up in trees are a fact of life in small-stream fishing. Get used to it.

Small-stream fishing is often spectacular in the middle of the day, when large rivers seem lifeless.

atures do fluctuate so that terrestrial insects, the primary food of small-stream trout, are more abundant in the middle of the day. Trout in small streams can and do respond to aquatic insect hatches, but this daily fluctuation of hatches is less pronounced in small streams. The bottom line is that small-stream trout fishing does not have the "down times" that you see on famous trout rivers. The trout are always eager to feed—*especially* in the middle of the day.

FLOODS

There is nothing more frustrating to a fly fisher than high water. It discourages trout from feeding on the surface, it is difficult to get your fly down to fish at the bottom of deep pools, and if the water is dirty it only magnifies the inability of a trout to find your fly. Luckily, small streams flood less often than big rivers and their floods are often discouraging but not a total catastrophe. Small streams don't always get dirty when their waters rise, so at most you have to deal with several inches to perhaps two feet of additional water in the stream channel, plus an increased current flow. In fact, when torrential rains flood popular trout streams, smart anglers head for tributaries and headwater streams even if they don't particularly care for small-stream fishing. Even to those who only look for big trout, small trout are better than none at all.

This difference means that, at most, you might have to tie on a nymph with a tungsten bead at its head or add a couple of split shot to your leader instead of walking away from the water shaking your head in disgust. In big rivers, high water usually means the end of dry-fly fishing because a trout that was lying in two feet of water, where it was an easy slide to the surface to pluck a bug from the film, might suddenly be covered by four additional feet of turbid flow. In a small stream, a few extra inches of water will still allow trout to see your dry fly, although you may have to find quieter pockets of water off to the side of the main flow. This is the time to fish a big size 8 or 10 dry fly. Trout in the small stream you are fishing may never see a large stonefly like a golden

Submerged streamside vegetation tells you when a river is higher than normal.

stone or a giant mayfly like a green drake, but they will rise to one if it looks remotely like food.

It's important to determine if a stream is higher than normal because it prevents you from fishing places that might be barren of fish. The best indicator is foliage along the edges of the stream. Once spring plants begin to grow in the early season, certain types will thrive right at the edge of the water and will continue to grow there throughout the season. Few will grow underwater, so if you see a patch of wild mint or young willow shoots with stems underwater, you can immediately tell the creek is in flood, and you can even tell how much higher than normal by the amount of stem underwater.

A trout chooses a place in a stream that protects it from current even at lower flows, and when the water rises from a rainstorm, the place that the fish has chosen doesn't get much faster. The water on the surface moves at a much faster pace than at normal flows, but the flow close to the bottom and near obstructions stays about the same because of the friction between objects and the flow. What a rise in water does is place an extra layer of velocity and depth between your offering and the fish, but a fish is quite content to ride it out in the same place, perhaps even more content, because floods wash addi-

tional terrestrial food like worms into a stream and high water often stimulates aquatic insect hatches.

So in high flows, imagine where trout would be lying at normal flows, and try to imagine what the brook looked like before the flood. If a small stream is a foot higher than normal, pockets that look great right now might have been almost dry a few days ago, and chances are trout have not moved into them, but stayed in the same places they were at low water. It's more difficult to get a trout to rise to a dry in high flows and it is harder to get a nymph down to its level, but by fishing in these tougher places at least you will be placing your fly where a trout may be living.

■ DROUGHTS

Droughts scare me because of their long-term effect on the health of small streams. They expose more fish to predators because as a stream channel shrinks there are fewer places for a trout to hide. A drought in the spring or fall spawning season can affect the spawning success of fish. Some small streams literally disappear if the water table gets too low. But I have to confess to you, fly fishing small streams during a drought can be superb, especially dry-fly fishing.

During a drought (or during normal low-water periods, for that matter), there will be little doubt where the fish are. They'll be in the deepest water in each pool, right under the main current flow. Watch the bubble line as it progresses through a pool and always place your fly along that narrow

Fly line selection is simple for small-stream fishing: all you need is a floating line. Small streams are never deep enough to require a sinking line, and even the deepest pools can be fished with a floating line and a tungsten-head nymph. Besides, nearly all small-stream fishing is done with dry flies. It's not even necessary to worry about whether to buy a weight-forward or double-taper line, because these lines are the same for the first 30 feet, and it will be a rare day when a 40-foot cast is needed. A double-taper line does offer one advantage, though. Because these lines are the same at both ends, when one end of the line wears out it's a simple matter of reversing the line on the spool to get a whole new, fresh line. Fly line finishes do wear out over the course of a few years, and lines used on small streams wear out quicker because they are constantly getting stepped on in shallow water or dragged across rocks, which shortens the life of a line.

FLY REELS

The choice of a fly reel for small-stream fishing is mostly a matter of aesthetics. Small-stream trout are seldom big enough to pull any line off the reel, so the need for a strong drag is minimal. There may be times when a fish bigger than expected is caught, and a large trout in a small stream may pull some line from the reel, but it usually has no place to run so the battle takes place within the confines of a small pool rather than along a stretch of river, eliminating the need for all but the lightest drag. An old-fashioned single-action reel with a click drag is all that is needed, and although most fly reels sold today come with strong disc drags, this feature isn't required on small streams.

The one consideration is whether to buy a narrow-arbor reel or one with a large-arbor spool. Although traditional arbor reels are small and light and seem to fit into the small-stream environment better, a case can be made for a large-arbor reel, with

its faster retrieve. The fast retrieve is not needed to fight fish, but in small streams it's common to walk between pools, and dragging a fly line along the ground instead of winding it onto the reel between spots is a sure way to get the line caught in branches and rocks. A large-arbor reel gets line back onto the reel faster, so less time will be spent reeling in line between each pool.

LEADERS AND TIPPET

With the short casts most often made in small streams, a short leader is less air resistant and will make casts easier and more accurate. In fast pocket water, where fish are not spooky and most drifts are very short anyway, a six-and-a-half-foot leader is perfect. With shorter rods, using a short leader also keeps the line-to-leader knot outside of the guides when landing a fish so there is less struggling. In bigger pools and low-gradient streams, where the water surface is smoother and trout can be wary, a seven-and-a-half-foot leader is often a smarter choice as it keeps the heavy fly line farther away from the fish, but is still short enough to straighten well on short casts. In the long, flat pools sometimes found in small streams, especially in flat meadow streams, where fish feed in clear, shallow water, a nine-foot leader might be needed.

I've experimented with braided and furled leaders on small streams, thinking that these more supple leaders would turn over better on short casts. Although they work well for delicate presentations on flat water in larger rivers, I've found that they don't push the bigger air-resistant dry flies most often used on small streams. The best leaders I've found are standard nylon knotless leaders with their stiffer butt sections.

Tippet sizes should correspond to the fly sizes used on small streams, and that usually means tippets from 3X to 6X. It's best to lean toward heavier tippets because the stronger ones make it easier to dislodge a fly from the overhanging branches that inevitably

clutch at flies no matter how carefully casts are made. Fish in small streams seldom break the tippet so its tempting to go to the lighter ones, but an extra couple of pounds of breaking strength can save you a half dozen flies over the course of a day. On larger trout rivers, fishing over selective fish, I often add fluorocarbon tippets, with their lower visibility, to a nylon leader. In small streams, however, a high-floating dry fly is critical, and fluorocarbon sinks quicker than nylon, so I avoid them as

I find they pull my fly under more often than a standard nylon tippet.

■ WADING GEAR

One of the great pleasures of small-stream fishing is that in warmer weather the streams can be fished without waders at all. You seldom get wet deeper than your knees, and because long walks are often involved, it's a pleasure to be unencumbered by waders. In meadow streams and lowland creeks without slippery rocks, even special wading shoes are unnecessary, and any comfortable footwear that can get wet—from sneakers to sandals—simplifies life even more. The one

You might be tempted to wear hip boots in a small stream, but you never know when you may have to cross in deep, fast water.

A wading staff can be just as much a lifesaver in small streams as it is in big rivers.

temptation that should usually be avoided is to wear shorts. Regardless of the temperature, biting bugs are often thick on small streams, especially black flies in the northern regions, and climbing around on rocks and scrambling through brush in shorts is no fun for most anglers. A better choice is a pair of lightweight, quick-drying hiking pants that protect from the elements but keep you cool; synthetic fabrics, especially nylon, are tougher and dry quicker than cotton.

When wading "wet" (without waders) in streams with slippery rocks, it's best to wear a pair of wading boots with rubber soles and metal studs. Small-stream anglers often move from one watershed to another and the chance of spreading invasive organisms like whirling disease, mud snails, and didymo is magnified. Rubber-soled wading shoes are easier to clean than felt soles when moving between watersheds, and rubber soles also make hiking on land easier than felt soles. Metal studs make rubber-soled wading shoes as secure as felt on slippery rocks, and in pocket-water streams with big boulders, a tumble into the shallow water of a tiny brook is more dangerous than a fall in a big river. Falling in a big river usually means just getting wet, but a fall on a small stream can mean a bruised or broken bone.

If the water is too cold to wade "wet" comfortably, chest- or waist high waders are surprisingly better suggestions than hip boots. Cold water usually means high water, and I find that no matter how shallow a stream appears, it's guaranteed that I'll go over the tops of my hip boots at least once, crossing the stream or wading into deeper water to retrieve a fly. Small-stream angling often requires a low-profile approach, and most fly fishers spend as much time on their knees as standing upright. Wearing hip boots while sneaking up on a trout on your knees is a sure way to spend the day with wet pants.

Don't rule out the use of a wading staff on small streams. We usually think of them as essential for fast, rushing rivers, but scrambling through slippery, rounded boulders—even if the water is only inches deep—can be just as tricky, and although you might not need a wading staff for balance in heavy current in small streams, it can make your day safer and more pleasant. Because it's unlikely that your staff will float away when you put it down in small streams, you can always find a stout stick as an alternative, placing it on a nearby rock when making a cast.

CLOTHING

There are no special rules for clothing when small-stream fishing. Wear what is comfortable, bearing in mind how far you'll walk and how long you'll be gone. Afternoon showers are common during the summer and even though you may start out in the early morning with not a cloud in the sky, by early afternoon storms could move in and make the second half of your day soggy if you don't pack a light raincoat.

Clothing color, however, is important. Small-stream fishing is at an intimate level, often with the angler 15 feet or less from the fish, so clothing that flashes against the background is just one more thing that might warn trout of your presence. Take a good look at the background foliage before you put on a shirt—if it's early spring and foliage is bare and brown, a medium brown or tan shirt will make you less visible against the background. In spring and summer, olive or green is best. When fishing a meadow stream where you're silhouetted against the sky, a light blue shirt might be your smartest move, but bear in mind that blue is one of the most attractive colors to biting insects. Camouflage clothing is not a bad idea; the colors blend into the background and the random shapes will break up your profile and further help with keeping your large predator profile less obvious. If you decide to go with a camouflage shirt, pick one designed for turkey hunting, as clothing designed for waterfowling is more suited to blending in with fall marshes and not woodland foliage.

Hats help keep the sun's glare out of your eyes and add some protection against biting insects. Pick one with a medium-sized brim with a dark underside to help prevent glare under the hat, because light reflected from the underside of a light hat brim can bounce around inside sunglasses and lower the clarity of vision.

FLY BOXES AND ESSENTIAL GEAR

It's a pleasure to take only one fly box on a day of small-stream fishing, so that box should be chosen carefully. It should be a box that has enough headroom for large dry flies, plus secure holders for weighted nymphs and streamers, which tend to shake loose because of their weight. Slotted foam boxes are lightweight and hold all kinds of flies securely. Properly designed slotted boxes have enough room to hold a big hackled dry fly without crushing it and are secure enough to hold weighted nymphs without letting them shake loose.

Forceps are essential for small-stream fishing. Small trout are more delicate and more easily injured than big river trout, so the ability to carefully remove a fly from a deeply hooked fish makes using forceps a responsible choice. Forceps also remove the barb from hooks quickly, and with a barbless hook, most trout can be shaken loose without ever having to touch the fish, the best way to ensure their survival.

Because most small-stream fishing is with a dry fly, at least two kinds of fly floatant should be carried at all times. First, a paste of liquid floatant is used to treat each dry fly before it touches the water. (You can also use this to grease your leader to keep it float-

A sling pack stays out of the way until you need something, then it can be brought around in front to dig out the perfect fly or new spool of tippet.

ing when fishing pocket water, a trick that helps reduce drag on the fly.) A water-repellent fly is one that will float longer and will eliminate the need to change flies as often. But you should always carry a second type of floatant, the kind made from a dry white powder. Once a fly begins to lose its water-proof qualities, and all flies will even with the best fly floatant, you can't re-treat a dry fly with paste, as all that does is gum up the fly. The white powder floatants re-treat a drowned fly by sucking all the moisture out of it, leaving a thin film of dry silicone on the outside of the fly. I feel crippled on a small stream if I forget or lose my bottle of this stuff.

And, of course, you'll need a few extra spools of tippet material and something to trim your knots. I think you can fish any small stream in the world with just 4X, 5X, and 6X tippet, which gives you the basic small-stream tippet size (5X), plus 4X in case you decide to fish a streamer or a big nymph and 6X for fishing still pools or beaver ponds with small flies.

■ OTHER GEAR YOU MIGHT WANT

During warm weather, a small thermometer can tell you when the water is too warm and it's time to move upstream or find a spring that offers cooler water and more comfort to the fish. Although the nice thing about most small streams is that you can use a dry-dropper combination instead of strike indicators and split shot because the water is shallow, on deeper streams and in the early season you might want to carry a few small indicators and some split shot or sink putty to get down into the deeper pools. If the water types you fish range from still pools to pocket water, it's a good idea to carry a six-foot, seven-and-a-half-foot, and nine-foot leader, although to keep tackle light it's possible to start with a six-foot leader and just add longer tippets on flat water.

■ CARRYING YOUR STUFF

How you carry your flies, water bottle, raincoat, and tackle depends entirely upon how minimal you want to go and how long your expedition is. For a few hours of fishing, many anglers stick one fly box and a couple of spools of tippet material into a pocket and clip a pair of forceps to the front of their shirt. For an all-day expedition, consider a small backpack that holds snacks, raincoat, GPS, camera, and other essentials. You can keep your fly box and tippet in a pocket, thus eliminating the need to take off the backpack every time you need to change flies.

Most small stream anglers pick an in-between plan. A vest, chest pack, waist pack, or sling bag will hold most of what you need for several hours, and there are considerations for each of them. A vest will carry more fly boxes and gadgets than you really need on a small stream, but if you're the type that likes to carry lots of gear, a vest can be a practical choice. Most people opt for either a chest pack or a waist pack because they get in the way less than a fully loaded vest, especially when hiking a lot or crawling around on rocks and in the brush. Chest packs carry more gear than waist packs, but many anglers find them annoying because they are always right in front and can be almost as annoying as a vest. Waist packs stay out of the way better, but if you do any deep wading there is a risk of getting your gear wet. A third alternative, my favorite, is a bag called a sling pack, which goes over your shoulder and can be slipped around in front to grab gear, then rotated behind your back to get it out of the way. I can get two fly boxes, all my tippet material and fly floatant, a small camera, and a few granola bars in my sling pack.

If you want to keep tools and tippet material out of the pockets of your bag or pack, consider getting a lanyard. You can hang snips, fly floatant, forceps, tippet spools, and even a small fly box on a lanyard, and some even come with a tubular foam fly patch to hold the patterns you need most often. On small streams, it's important to get a lanyard with a clip that keeps it tight to your shirt, not hanging loose at the bottom, because in this kind of fishing you'll be bending over a lot while sneaking up on trout.

PARACHUTE ADAMS

SIZES: 12–18

TAIL: Mixed brown and grizzly hackle fibers

BODY: Gray fur, typically muskrat

WING: White calf tail or calf body hair

HACKLE: Mixed brown and grizzly, parachute-style

NOTES: The most popular dry fly of all time, the Parachute Adams is a staple in small streams. It seems to imitate many different insects and is as good in the smallest sizes in flat water in the summer as it is in bigger sizes in the early season and in pocket water.

PARACHUTE HARE'S EAR

SIZES: 10–16

TAIL: Brown bucktail, short and heavy

BODY: Dark hare's ear fur

WING: White calf body hair, thick

HACKLE: Brown and grizzly, heavy parachute-style

NOTES: This fly is very similar to the Parachute Adams, but is bulkier, floats better, and is more visible because of its heavier wing and dense hackle. It is an excellent fly in pocket water and fast riffles.

ADAMS

SIZES: 12–18

TAIL: Mixed brown and grizzly hackle fibers

BODY: Gray fur, typically muskrat

WING: Two wide grizzly hackle tips

HACKLE: Mixed brown and grizzly

NOTES: Sometimes, especially in fast water, the standard hackled version of the Adams works better than the parachute version, although it is not as easy to see. It is especially good if insects are fluttering on the water.

STIMULATOR

SIZES: 8–18

TAIL: Light elk, flared wide

BODY: Fluorescent yellow Antron ribbed with grizzly hackle and fine gold wire

WING: Light elk, flared wide and tied so it sticks up high

HACKLE: Grizzly tied over a thorax of amber goat hair or other dubbing

NOTES: The bulk of this fly, combined with its high-profile wing, keeps it visible to both fish and anglers. It imitates a stonefly or grasshopper, but is also just a great pattern when fish are attracted to a large dry fly. Designed by Randall Kaufmann for fishing western rivers, it is equally deadly in small streams throughout the world.

AUSABLE WULFF

SIZES: 10–16

TAIL: Brown bucktail or moose body hair, heavy
The original pattern called for woodchuck tail hair, but this material is often hard to find.

BODY: Tan fur dubbed on hot orange thread
The original version called for Australian opossum.

WING: White calf tail, upright and divided

HACKLE: Mixed brown and grizzly

NOTES: Like most great small-stream flies, this pattern has a mixed, buggy look that can imitate many different insects. Developed by Francis Betters for the Adirondack Mountains of New York, it is best in fast water.

ROYAL WULFF

SIZES: 10–18

TAIL: Brown bucktail

BODY: Peacock herl with a band of red floss in the center

WING: White calf tail or calf body hair
The original pattern used white bucktail, which sheds water better but is more difficult to use.

HACKLE: Brown, heavy

NOTES: The great Lee Wulff modified the traditional Royal Coachman fly into a fast-water attractor in the 1930s, and it is still very popular today. It probably imitates many different types of terrestrial insects as well as dark aquatic insects.

PARACHUTE BEETLE

SIZES: 12–18

TAIL: None

BODY: Green sparkle dubbing with an overlay of black foam

WING: Can be made from white or bright-colored foam, calf body hair, or synthetic yarn

HACKLE: Black, parachute-style

NOTES: Beetles land with more disturbance than ants and this pattern will sometimes draw trout from deep, slow water when ant patterns and traditional dry flies don't work. Like the Parachute Ant, it is best in slower water.

PARACHUTE ANT

SIZES: 14–20

TAIL: None

BODY: Two lumps of black fur with a narrow band in the middle

WING: White calf body hair (or another highly visible color like orange or bright red), tied in the middle of the hook

HACKLE: Black, parachute-style

NOTES: There are times when a low-floating ant pattern may work to the exclusion of all other flies, as trout seldom refuse an ant. This pattern is best for flat water as it does not float as well as other dry flies and is more difficult to see.

PARACHUTE HOPPER

SIZES: 8–12

TAIL: None

BODY: Tan fur for both abdomen and thorax

WING: Mottled turkey wing quill fiber, treated with a spray fixative or vinyl cement and tied flat over the body; knotted legs made from pheasant tail fibers are placed along both sides of the wing

HACKLE: Mixed brown and grizzly, tied parachute-style

NOTES: Although the Stimulator is fine for imitating larger grasshoppers and the Elk Hair Caddis looks like small nymph hoppers, where these insects are abundant trout sometimes get quite selective. The Parachute Hopper is a very accurate imitation of a grasshopper, plus it floats well and is more visible than any other grasshopper pattern.

YELLOW HUMPY

SIZES: 12–18

TAIL: Light elk hair

BODY: Yellow tying thread built up to a bulky shape with an overlay of light elk hair

WING: Light elk hair

HACKLE: Mixed brown and grizzly

NOTES: A great midsummer fly when light-colored mayflies and caddis flies hatch. Its bulky profile also makes it a reasonable imitation for beetles and other terrestrial insects.

ELK HAIR CADDIS

SIZES: 10–18

TAIL: None

BODY: Tan fur ribbed with brown hackle

WING: Tan elk hair, with butt ends left exposed to form the head

HACKLE: None

NOTES: The Elk Hair Caddis imitates the caddis flies abundant on all trout streams and it floats well and is easy to see on the water. It also imitates moths, small grasshoppers, and other terrestrial insects. It can be tied with many different body colors, but the tan version seems to work just fine on small streams.

SPARKLE DUN

SIZES: 14–20

TAIL: Antron yarn to match body

BODY: Olive, tan, rusty, yellow, or gray fur

WING: Coastal deer hair tied upright and flared 180 degrees across the upper body

HACKLE: None

NOTES: There may be times when small-stream fish feed selectively on emerging mayflies. Although it is rare for them to be as selective as trout in bigger rivers, the Sparkle Dun will fool trout in any river, big or small, when mayflies are hatching. Its advantage on small streams is that it floats well and is easy to see. To match any possible mayfly have all the colors mentioned here in your box, but the two absolute essentials are the olive and yellow.

HARE'S EAR

SIZES: 8–18

TAIL: Brown hackle fibers, short and webby

ABDOMEN: Dark hare's ear fur ribbed with oval gold tinsel

THORAX: Hare's ear fur, tied heavy and picked out at the sides to imitate legs

WING CASE: Wide strip from a duck wing quill

LEGS: None

NOTES: The most popular nymph of all time, the Hare's Ear imitates a host of different insects and crustaceans. In the bigger sizes it matches small crayfish, large flat mayflies, and stoneflies; in the smaller sizes it is probably mistaken by trout for a caddis larva, smaller mayflies, midge pupae, and drowned terrestrials.

BEADHEAD HARE'S EAR

SIZES: 8–16

TAIL: Brown hackle fibers, short and webby

ABDOMEN: Dark hare's ear fur ribbed with oval gold tinsel

THORAX: Gold bead, brass for a medium sink rate, and tungsten bead for a fast sink rate and deeper pools

WING CASE: None

LEGS: None

NOTES: This fly adds flash and weight to the standard Hare's Ear. It seems to work best in deeper, faster water, especially when caddis flies are seen on the water.

PHEASANT TAIL

SIZES: 14–18

TAIL: Pheasant tail fibers

ABDOMEN: Pheasant tail fibers wound and ribbed with fine copper wire

THORAX: Wound pheasant tail fibers

WING CASE: None

LEGS: None

NOTES: This slim, subtle nymph works well when traditional, bulkier flies don't produce. It imitates small mayfly nymphs, small stoneflies, and midge larvae and pupae. It works best in slow, clear water when bigger flies and beadheads frighten the trout.

PRINCE

SIZES: 10–16

TAIL: Brown turkey or goose wing biots

ABDOMEN: None

THORAX: None

BODY: Peacock herl ribbed with fine, flat gold tinsel

WING CASE: Two white turkey or goose wing biots tied over entire body of the fly

LEGS: Brown hackle

NOTES: The Prince is a fly that, like the Hare's Ear, imitates a wide variety of aquatic insects but most anglers consider it a stonefly imitation. Like the other nymphs listed here, it has many variations and is often tied with a brass or tungsten bead for added flash and weight.

BEADHEAD PHEASANT TAIL

SIZES: 14–18

TAIL: Pheasant tail fibers

ABDOMEN: Pheasant tail fibers wound and ribbed with fine copper wire

THORAX: Small copper bead, or copper-plated tungsten for deeper water

WING CASE: Bunch of pheasant tail fibers

LEGS: None

NOTES: The Beadhead Pheasant Tail is best for deeper, faster water where small mayflies or stoneflies are abundant.

PARTRIDGE AND ORANGE SOFT-HACKLE

SIZES: 10–16

TAIL: None

ABDOMEN: Hare's ear fur tied slightly thicker than the abdomen

THORAX: Orange floss tied thin

WING CASE: None

LEGS: Brown partridge wound as a collar, very sparse

NOTES: The sparse nature of this fly makes it a perfect wet fly for swinging over fish in shallow water. It works best when caddis flies are on the water, but is also good whenever it's necessary to fish downstream.

CAREY SPECIAL

SIZES: 10–16

TAIL: Pheasant tail fibers

ABDOMEN: Peacock herl ribbed with copper wire

THORAX: None

WING CASE: None

LEGS: Pheasant tail fibers tied in and distributed around the fly so they encircle the body like hackle

NOTES: Great for imitating caddis fly, dragonfly, and damselfly larvae, this nymph works anywhere, but is deadly in slower bog rivers and beaver ponds where these insects are common.

BEADHEAD HARE'S EAR SOFT-HACKLE

SIZES: 12–16

TAIL: Brown partridge fibers

ABDOMEN: Brass bead

THORAX: Hare's ear fur ribbed with fine gold wire

WING CASE: None

LEGS: Brown partridge wound in front of the bead as a collar

NOTES: This fly is best fished downstream, swung on a tight line, in faster riffles and deeper pools.

Streamers

BLACK NOSE DACE

SIZES: 8–14

TAIL: Red wool, short (or red thread on Mylar version)

BODY: Flat silver tinsel ribbed with oval silver tinsel, or fine silver Mylar tubing

WING: Sparse brown over black over white bucktail, in three distinct bands

NOTES: Although baitfish are not abundant in many small streams, the Black Nose Dace does live alongside trout in headwater streams. This small, sparse streamer is perfect for imitating them, and it is subtle enough not to frighten trout that would be spooked by larger streamers.

MICKEY FINN

SIZES: 8–12

TAIL: None

BODY: Flat silver tinsel ribbed with oval silver tinsel, or fine silver Mylar tubing

WING: Yellow over red over yellow bucktail, in three distinct bands

NOTES: In tiny first-order streams, where trout don't see flies very often, a bright fly like the Mickey Finn is sometimes a great attractor pattern. This streamer is especially good for wilderness brook trout and cutthroats.

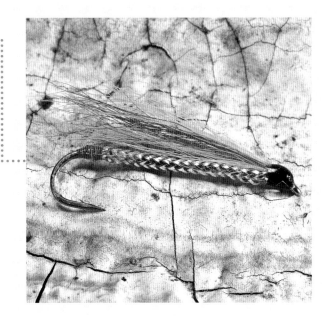

BEADHEAD WOOLLY BUGGER

SIZES: 8–14

TAIL: Black Marabou

BODY: Olive chenille palmered with black hackle

WING: None

BEAD: Brass

NOTES: The Beadhead Woolly Bugger is another good fly when the water is too high or dirty to fish standard dries and nymphs. This is a fly to drag through a deep, dark pool after other flies have failed to produce a rise.

CONEHEAD YELLOW MARABOU MUDDLER

SIZES: 10–14

TAIL: Red hackle fibers

BODY: Flat gold tinsel ribbed with oval gold tinsel

WING: Yellow Marabou topped with three strands of peacock herl

HEAD AND COLLAR: Deer hair, spun and trimmed

CONE: Brass or brass-plated tungsten for deeper water

NOTES: This is a good fly for higher water and off-color creeks in flood. It is better in the lower reaches of small streams, where more baitfish, especially sculpins, are found.

 **Chapter 6** ....

Casting in Small Streams

Because this is a book about small-stream fly fishing and not basic fly casting, I'm assuming some level of casting ability on your part. You should at least know the basic motions of the overhead cast and roll cast, and how to mend line. If you're comfortable with those basic elements of fly casting you should be able to follow any of the advice in this chapter. If not, I suggest you get some basic casting lessons from an instructor, a book, or a video, which will make this chapter a lot clearer and should enable you to take those basic skills and fine-tune them for the special challenges we face on small streams.

A Philosophy of Small-Stream Casting

A good small-stream fly fisher is, if nothing else, efficient. Casts are short, quick, and designed to avoid streamside brush, and they don't always look as elegant as casts in big, wide-open trout streams or steelhead rivers. Watching a small-stream expert at work makes you think he or she is cavalier about getting hung up in the brush and losing flies, but often the best spots are the ones close to cover where most anglers just give up in frustration or worry about losing a fly. To be really successful in these tiny waters, you can't have an anxiety attack over losing a few flies—and anyway in a small creek a fly never gets hung up in brush that can't be approached, unlike in bigger rivers where you might lose a fly over a deep hole on the far bank or way up in a tall tree. You never cast that far in a small stream.

The best cast in a small stream is not some tricky cast reserved for brush fishing. It's a standard overhead cast, and it's surprising to find, once you begin wading upstream, how much room you have

PAGES 134–135: Short, accurate casts, without false casts, are the essence of small-stream fly fishing.

OPPOSITE: Besides the rare wide-open pool, casting in small streams should be short and tight.

behind you and in front of you, even if the banks are as thick as a tropical rain forest. The overhead cast is more powerful, more accurate, and easier than any other cast as long as you have moderate clearance.

Don't fire a 30-foot cast to the head of a pool on a small stream when a 15-foot one will do the same job. It's much better to sneak up on a spot and make a short, accurate cast than it is to throw a long line over the entire pool, doubling the chances that the fly will hang up in a tree or the line will land on top of several fish between you and your target. A leader falling on top of a trout seldom spooks it; the heavier, opaque fly line, however, lands with a much bigger splash and is almost guaranteed to send all those fish sprinting to the head for protection, spooking any fish at your intended target as well. One fish streaking through a pool will often telegraph an alarm by its quick movements because the other fish sense that something is wrong.

If you watch a polished small-stream junky, especially in tiny plunge pools or pocket water, you'll often see him or her work with only three or four feet of fly line outside of the tip-top of the rod, and the line itself never touches the water. A quick cast is made with a single back and then forward stroke. The rod tip is raised to keep all of the line off the water—only the leader hits the water. They follow the progress of the fly by raising the rod higher and higher until it gets to just below the rod tip, and the fly is then flicked back for another cast with the same simple motion.

False casts are the bane of small-stream angling. The more your fly loops through the air, the greater the chance you *will* get hung up, so do everything you can to keep false casts at a minimum. False casting the thick fly line also creates movement that spooks trout. They don't know what the bright yellow string flying through the air is, but you can bet they don't think for a second it is something good for their long-term health.

One of the best ways to prevent the need for extra false casts is to clean fly lines often, after every fishing trip. A clean fly line shoots better, and by shooting line that has been stripped in during a drift, line can be fired back into the cast with a single forward stroke because it shoots through the guides better. It also helps to straighten the line at the beginning of each outing by pulling three feet of line from the reel at a time, then pulling the line between your hands until it stretches slightly. This will smooth out the loops in the line that develop as it is stored on the arbor of a fly reel.

When you do need to make a 20-foot cast, strip enough line off the reel and let it lie at your feet. Try to coil it carefully if you are standing on rocks or gravel, or hold it in loose loops if you are wading. Make a single cast and shoot all of the line on your one forward stroke. If the line is clean and the kinks have been pulled out of it, and if it is looped properly, you'll find you can shoot 10 or 15 feet with a single cast. As the line drifts back to you during the fly's drift, again try to coil the line carefully. When the line to leader junction is five feet off the rod tip, pick up, make a single backcast, and again shoot all the line without a false cast. You may find the need to dry the fly occasionally with a few short false casts, but you will be amazed at how little you need to false cast and still get the distance and keep your fly floating. Try to false cast with only five feet of line, off to one side and not directly over the fish (or where you think a fish is) to prevent spooking it.

If you make a bad cast on a small stream, the worst thing is to rip the line off the water to make another one. First, yanking line off the water immediately after the cast means disturbing all that water. Let the cast fish out. Let it drift out of productive territory before trying again. A line quietly drifting over a fish *might* spook it, but a line yanked off the water on top of a fish will remove all doubt. Besides, I've caught more nice trout than I can count on bad casts, and your fly is always better in the water than waving through the air.

No-Cast Solutions

▪ DAPPING

There may be times when a cast is not appropriate or even possible. Getting a fly into a small hole in the brush where even the tightest loop would hang up is one example. So is creeping up behind a boulder in the tail of a pool and seeing a trout lying right in front of the rock. You might argue that in a spot like this second example, the best approach would be to sneak around in front of the rock and make a downstream cast to it. However, any additional commotion you make on a small stream risks spooking a fish, and many times you won't be able to creep upstream of a fish because streamside brush is very dense and your only route is up the middle of the stream.

Dapping is an age-old method of fishing, actually the precursor of modern fly fishing. In medieval times, anglers would impale a live fly to a hook, then use a long rod to position the bait in the vicinity of a trout and dip it gently on the water to imitate a mayfly striking the water repeatedly to lay its eggs. Once the fish took the bait it was merely winched around to the bank. Dapping with live mayflies is still practiced in Ireland today and probably in many other places.

Dapping with an artificial fly is not much different. It's accomplished by raising the rod tip slowly and gently to lessen the possibility that a trout will spook, as fast movements are much more frightening than slower movements, especially where branches kiss the water and trout are used to seeing

Sometimes just dapping the fly is the best approach.

long skinny objects slowly swaying in the breeze. The rod tip is then placed a few inches upstream of the fish and the fly is allowed to just barely kiss the water, and before the current pulls it downstream and causes drag, the fly is lifted a few inches into the air and then placed back on the surface. Trout will take the fly just as it hits the water and occasionally a fish will leap into the air and take the fly while it is still suspended. Neither the line nor the leader should touch the water when dapping—just the fly.

Longer rods are better than shorter rods for dapping because they keep you farther from the fish. If you fish places where dapping is often the only way to get a fly to a fish, stay away from rods under seven-and-a-half feet long. Of course a nine-foot or longer rod is the best tool for pure dapping, but in most tiny streams you alternate between short casts and dapping so a compromise is needed and most people prefer a rod of about eight feet long. This gives them a nice dapping tool in addition to a rod that is short enough to make overhead or roll casts when needed.

It's sometimes difficult to get a fly placed just where you want it when dapping, especially with a breeze. You can handle this two ways. One is to let the wind carry your fly to the fish and then manipulate the rod so that the fly alternates between drifting free in the breeze and touching the water briefly. With an upstream breeze, this gives you the advantage of keeping the rod behind the fish, in its blind spot, while the wind carries only the fly and the tippet in front of the fish. In tight spots, it's sometimes tough to thread that air-resistant fly into tunnels in the brush without tangling, and one way to avoid this and place the fly more accurately is to attach a split shot six inches above the fly on the tippet. The shot anchors the leader in a straight line between the rod tip and the fly so you can drop it into tight spots easier. Did you ever think you would be fishing a dry fly with a split shot?

■ JIGGING

One variation on dapping that utilizes a sinking fly and/or split shot doesn't really have an official fly-fishing name, but I call it jigging. It's basically worm fishing with a fly. If you have a spot with a tiny pool or undercut bank with no room for a backcast and no room for a drift either, you can dap a weighted nymph or streamer into the hole in the brush, letting it sink toward the bottom by lowering the rod tip, and then raising the rod tip while gently twitching it. In the stream I describe in the introduction to this book, I started out fishing worms because I thought it was the only way to get something down under the logjams and undercut banks that were surrounded by brush. I later graduated to a size 12 weighted White Marabou streamer and jigged it in the same manner as I did my worms. It wasn't nearly as effective, but at least I could say I was fishing with a fly!

■ FEEDING LINE DOWNSTREAM

You may encounter a place where a log has fallen completely across a stream and there is no possible way to make a presentation from a downstream angle and limited space upstream of the obstruction as well. You might also find a spot where a tunnel of brush has grown over the surface, making it impossible to present a fly close to where you think the fish are feeding. In both cases, creep carefully upstream of the obstruction. Get into a position where you can at least flip a few feet of line onto the water. Get a few feet of line outside of the rod tip, even if you only have enough room to pull it manually through the guides. Strip enough line from the reel to reach down to the log or into the tunnel of brush and keep it coiled neatly in your line hand. Get the line onto the water in front of you any way you can—with an abbreviated roll cast or by making repeated sideways

OPPOSITE: In tight spots, feeding line downstream may be your only solution.

flips of the rod until you get at least a couple of feet of line on the water. Mend the line until the fly is positioned upstream of where you want it to drift, then point the rod tip straight downstream and wiggle it gently from side to side to allow the loose line in your hand to slide through the guides.

As in all small-stream fishing, you'll have an advantage if your line is clean and slick and the kinks have been stretched out before you begin. The line you first placed on the water will pull the line through the guides, and with good preparation you can feed a fly up to 10 feet under an obstruction before it begins to drag.

This technique can be used with any kind of fly—dry, nymph, wet, or streamer. However, because drag usually ruins a presentation with a dry fly and fish don't seem to mind it with a subsurface fly, the best use of the downstream drift is with a streamer or nymph. With a dry fly, once the line straightens at the end of the drift you're done. But with a subsurface fly, you then retrieve the fly back to you with short strips and trout may take the fly both as it drifts downstream (watch for a tightening of the line) or on the retrieve.

Variations on the Forward Cast

◼ GETTING WRISTY AND CHOKED UP

We've been taught all our lives to keep wrist movement at a minimum when making an overhead cast, using the forearm for most of the motion and the wrist for the final acceleration. This is fine advice on big rivers and in saltwater because it provides the needed power and a longer casting arc for developing more power. But on really short casts the forearm is not only unnecessary, it's a hindrance. Using the forearm makes the rod tip travel through a longer arc, just what is needed on long casts, but on small brushy streams a longer arc sometimes means a blown cast when the fly gets hung up in the branches.

Using mostly wrist with little forearm is what casting schools tell you not to do. But in small streams, it keeps your casting arc short and tight and out of trouble.

If you're forced into a green tunnel with little room to make a cast, keeping the forearm close to your body and just using the wrist works fine. As long as you keep the backcast parallel to the water—in other words don't "break your wrist" on the backcast so that the rod tip dumps the line behind you—it's possible to fish all day long using very little forearm. It's a little more tiring because your wrist muscles aren't as strong as your forearm muscles, but on the short casts needed on small streams your wrist muscles should hold up just fine.

If keeping the forearm close to your body still doesn't provide enough clearance for a cast, there is one additional way to shorten the casting arc: by choking up on the rod. Sure, it's more comfortable to cast with the cork grip on a rod, but for the occasional very tight cast bring your casting hand six inches or even a foot up on the butt section of the rod. It feels strange because the balance point of the reel works against you, but that extra foot of space could mean the difference between making a presentation and moving on to find an easier spot.

SIDE CAST

Small-stream fishing invariably gets you into tight spots, but it's surprising how much added casting room you can get by merely changing your position. Right-handed casters working upstream (the way most small streams are approached) should always try to work along the left side of a small stream, because all comfortable casting motions take place on the right side of the body, and even with a nearly vertical overhead cast some line leaks off to the right side of the rod. Direct overhead casts, with the rod sliced through a vertical plane in front of and behind the body, are the best casts in meadow streams with low brush on either side. However, in woodland streams, with trees overhead and brush along the banks, the best overhead cast is one that tips off to the right side, so that casting loops travel in a plane somewhere between 10 degrees off to the right side to completely horizontal, with the fly line remaining nearly parallel to the water throughout the cast.

Imagine you are a right-handed caster working upstream along the left bank of a 20-foot-wide woodland stream. Both banks are covered with small trees and brush, and occasional mature yellow birch trees spread their branches 10 feet above the water. Even with a very tight casting loop, a straight overhead cast will put your fly into the branches every time. The only casting room is off to your right side, over the middle of the stream.

The side cast is quite easy to perform and most casters develop a little sidearm motion naturally. However, to turn the overhead cast completely onto its side requires more concentration. Before casting, instead of the back of the wrist facing the right side, the entire wrist and forearm should rotate until the back of the wrist faces the surface of the

The side cast will keep your fly out of overhanging trees.

When working up the right side of a stream, a right-handed angler can cast across the front of his body. Note that his thumb will be on top at the completion of the cast, better for punchier casts and getting better distance.

water. Casting motions here should be a little more brisk than with a standard overhead cast. With the overhead cast, if you get a little sloppy or if the wind pushes the backcast down below the tip of the rod, you have some leeway. It won't always ruin the cast. However, with a side cast the line is no more than two or three feet above the surface, and any mistake catches the line on the water and ruins the cast. Thus, keeping the line in the air requires faster line speed and close attention to timing. Keeping the wrist and forearm at this casting angle also introduces fatigue because casting motions aren't as easy in this position.

Side casts are not only handy for casting in tight brush. Sometimes it's the only way to drive a fly under a branch hanging over the water ahead of you, or under a tuft of long grass at the edge of the bank. You might have room for a straight overhead cast where you are standing, but a casting loop that unfurls in a vertical plane won't get the fly under an obstruction. In that case you need a loop that curls in a horizontal plane, and with enough line speed that gravity doesn't take effect before the fly is driven under the obstruction. There is no cast other than an overhead cast turned on its side that will do this for you.

It's also easier to throw a curve cast with a side cast. Imagine a trout feeding in front of a big boulder as you work upstream through some pocket water. You can throw your cast right on top of the boulder (and sometimes that's a great idea to help avoid drag), but let's imagine the boulder is covered with moss and low brush so casting over it isn't possible. By making a side cast off to the right and pulling back slightly on the rod tip just before the line settles, the line will snap off to the left in a nice curve, dropping the fly in front of the boulder and the line off to the right side.

In the same situation, a right-handed angler can also make a cast behind and to his left side and then just dump his "backcast" in front. Note that his thumb will be on the bottom at the completion of this cast.

▨ TOWER CAST

In meadow streams or around beaver ponds, where low bushes or tall grasses present casting obstacles, it's important to keep the backcast very high. A fly rod eight-and-a-half feet or longer can help with this, but on small streams, when you move from a meadow area to a wooded spot, you get stuck with a rod that is longer than is practical. The tower cast keeps the backcast out of shoulder-height brush; I'm sure you can imagine that it's no fun slogging through 20 feet of alder swamp to retrieve a fly that has gone AWOL on the backcast.

To make a tower cast, begin with the rod tip right at the surface of the water. You're about to make an abbreviated backcast and you will need all the room you can get to load the rod, because the tip of the rod will never go behind your shoulder. With a brisk motion, even brisker than on a standard overhead cast, begin the backcast, but as you do, raise your entire arm as far above your head as you can and point the rod tip straight up into the air. The line will still continue on slightly behind you, but it should stay well clear of the brush as it will be about six feet higher than normal.

Because you've changed the angle of the cast from mostly back-and-forth to almost straight up-and-down, the challenge is to make a forward cast that doesn't slam the leader, fly, and line into a big puddle in front of you. The best way to avoid this is to put less drive into the forward cast; stop the cast higher than normal (about level with the top of your head) and just before the line hits the water pull back with your arm to attempt to take some of the downward energy out of the cast. This is not a great cast for distance and there is always the risk of slamming the line on the water and spooking fish, but with a wall of high grass behind you it's sometimes the only way.

The parachute cast begins by aiming the cast high in the air.

The line goes up in the air and snaps back.

■ CROSS-BODY CAST AND DUMPING THE BACKCAST

There will be times when right-handed casters need to cast close to the right bank when working upstream. Brush and trees extending out into the river corridor on the left side, or water along the left bank that is too deep to wade, are common reasons. If you can learn to cast with your left hand you can solve this problem, but most of us have enough trouble casting with our dominant hand, and if you've never tried it, trying to cast with the non-dominant hand is almost like learning to cast all over again. Never underestimate the importance of muscle memory.

If you fish small streams for long, you'll need to become one with some sort of cross-body cast, where a right-handed angler casts over the left shoulder. There are two ways to accomplish this. One is to keep the wrist at the normal position but cross your forearm and upper arm in front of your body. Like the side cast, this moves your arm into a position that is more tiring. Alternatively, you can turn your upper body around and make a cast behind you, dumping the "backcast" in front.

At first glance, this second approach seems to make more sense. Not only are you using a normal casting motion, but you can also check behind you for trees and brush that could catch the fly on the backcast. However, when dumping the backcast you'll notice that when you present the fly, the wrist has to bend backward at an uncomfortable angle. As a result, the cast is not as precise because it is more difficult to point the rod tip where you want the fly to land. The cross-body cast, on the other hand, presents the wrist at the normal position for the forward cast.

I recommend that you try both methods. From my experience, the cross-body cast is more precise but is better for short casts, so I use it in tight spots with a dry fly where I need to place my fly just right. Dumping the backcast is better for longer casts where exact placement of the fly is less important, so I use it more often for fishing streamers where the fly is cast into a deep pool and then worked back through the pool.

The rod is then immediately lowered straight down.

The line falls to the water in loose coils and the leader ends up with a large pile of slack that will help avoid drag.

◼ PARACHUTE CAST

Even though small-stream trout are not very fussy when deciding what fly to eat, wilderness brook trout are often as sensitive to drag on a dry fly as a hard-fished brown trout on a big river. A silly-looking fly that drifts like a natural insect is a lot safer gamble for a trout than a realistic fly that streaks across the surface like a motorboat. This is especially critical in pocket water, where a half dozen conflicting cross-currents may influence a line and leader on a single 20-foot cast. The parachute cast introduces extra slack line into a presentation, slack that adds extra insurance because all the coils and wrinkles must come out of the line before it straightens and affects the fly.

To make a parachute cast, begin an overhead cast as you normally would. On the forward cast, stop the rod tip just a couple degrees higher than normal and immediately drop your elbow straight down in the same motion kids use to get tractor-trailer drivers to blow their horns. Most of the fly line between you and the line will float to the water in loose curves instead of straightening, and as a result your fly will float drag-free throughout most of the drift, if not all of it.

The parachute cast requires room for an overhead cast (it doesn't work with a side cast because that cast is done so close to the water), but where you have the room and tricky currents abound, this cast is one of the most useful variations on the forward cast you'll see. There are other ways to avoid drag, like changing positions, curve casts, and adding a longer tippet, but for sheer utility the parachute cast works in nearly any situation, as long as you have overhead casting room.

Roll Cast

Most anglers think the roll cast is used more often than the overhead cast in small streams, but its utility is overrated, especially as compared to some of the tricks I've described so far. It's hard to make the roll cast as accurate as a short overhead or side cast, and accuracy is one of the prime tenets of small-stream trout fishing. It's true that the roll cast has no backcast, but in many small-stream situations there is plenty of room behind the angler as long as the entire stream does not burrow through impenetrable brush. And don't forget that the roll

cast still needs plenty of room in front of you to move the rod tip, just as much as with a standard overhead cast.

Where the roll cast really shines is when working downstream. With an upstream dry fly or nymph, casts stay parallel to the banks and over the middle of the stream. However, when working downstream with a streamer, nymph, or wet fly, the fly should be cast at an angle to the current so that it swings across the current in front of the fish. With brush behind you, it's often impossible to make even a short backcast, so here the roll cast is essential. When working downstream, trout are always facing you, so the less obvious your motions the better. A roll cast keeps the line lower to the water and is made with a minimum of rod motion so it is a very stealthy cast.

A roll cast can be made from a low position like a side cast but only in a limited manner. It requires a semicircle of line below the rod tip to function properly, and with the rod low to the water there is little leeway, so stick to short side casts with the roll cast. The roll cast can be made across the front of the body, though, and many anglers forget this. Just bring the rod slowly across the front of your body and make sure that the semicircle of line used to develop the roll is outside of the rod tip, not between the rod tip and your body, or you'll end up with a fly in your arm—or worse.

In very tight spots I'll often use a cross between a roll cast and an incomplete overhead cast with an abbreviated backcast. I don't even know if this cast has an official name, but it's great in a tight spot. Raise your rod tip as the fly drifts back toward you and make a quick circle with the tip of the rod, just enough to get the line moving. Then quickly go into a backcast, but don't let the line get very far behind you before you snap the rod forward to deliver the line. It doesn't look pretty and won't win you any admiring glances from other anglers on the river, but it works.

Snap-T Cast

My friend Bill Reed showed me a cast that is normally reserved for big two-handed rods, but is perfect in small streams as an alternative to the roll cast and gives you more distance—the snap-T. It is especially useful when you want to swing a fly across the current, but you have no room behind you to make a backcast. In this case the only direction you can cast is straight downstream, but that does not help you get the fly to the far bank in a tight spot. You might think that just a simple roll cast to the far bank will work, but this causes problems when the line is hanging downstream, because making a roll cast while trying to change directions often flips the fly onto your rod, or worse, into your anatomy. A snap-T will dump the line and fly on your upstream side so you can carefully make a roll cast.

Start this cast with the line dragging downstream below you. Raise the tip of the rod slowly in front of you and to the upstream side of your body. Then make a quick chopping motion with the rod tip, from this high upstream position to a low upstream spot, describing an arc with the open end facing up. The line will flip over the rod tip and then the leader, fly, and most of the line will dump on your upstream side, at which point you can rotate the rod off to your upstream side and make a normal roll cast.

Bill Reed demonstrates his small-stream snap-T cast. He begins with the line hanging downstream.

He rolls the rod from a high upstream position to a low downstream presentation.

The line and leader now fall on his upstream side.

He can now make a standard roll cast to fire the fly to the other side of the stream.

Standard Bow-and-Arrow Cast

If you fish tiny streams, sooner or later you'll find a need for the bow-and-arrow cast. Imagine you are fishing a tiny plunge pool with absolutely no backcast room and no room on either side—just a narrow channel down the middle of the brook. And the spot you want to hit is too far away to dap the fly, around twice the length of your rod, a situation that is very common if you fish a short rod in tight brush. While the bow-and-arrow cast is not very precise nor is it a cast of elegance or beauty, it is a cast that gets the fly into a tight spot with a minimum of motion, so not only is it a good cast for tight spots, it's a great cast for spooky fish.

To make a bow-and-arrow cast, pull enough line and leader outside of your rod tip so that you have a length slightly longer than the rod outside of the tip-top. Depending on the length of your rod and leader, this might be just leader and no fly line at all or you may have a foot or so of line outside of the tip-top. Either way is fine. Grab the fly in your fingertips at the bend of the hook so that when you launch the fly it does not impale your fingers. (If you hold it with the hook point facing up, this will further keep you out of trouble.) Pull back on the fly over the top of the rod while you pinch the fly line tight against the rod with your other hand, bending the rod tip back slightly. When you have pulled the fly back as far as you can reach, point the non-bent portion of the rod at the target and release the fly. The spring of the rod tip will drive the fly at its target, although only a rod length away.

Scott Farfone uses a standard bow-and-arrow cast in a North Carolina mountain stream.

The Joe Humphreys Bow-and-Arrow Cast

The legendary Joe Humphreys—from the State College, Pennsylvania, area—is one of the finest small-stream anglers I have ever seen. When I fished with him on a small Pennsylvania brook in 2010, he was 82 years old and still a canny and precise small-stream angler. One of the main reasons he is so much better on small streams is how well he can cast in tight spots, and he showed me a cast he developed as a teenager, a cast I had seen him do once in a demonstration but had never seen in print anywhere. He graciously showed me the tricks to his bow-and-arrow cast and allowed me to be the first writer to describe the technique.

Joe's bow-and-arrow cast doubles or even triples the distance you can reach with absolutely no back-cast. It requires less room than a roll cast and can be fired in tight spots. Joe's secret is that he coils and palms extra shooting line outside of the rod tip, and when the cast is done properly it's a thing of beauty. To make the Joe Humphreys bow-and-arrow cast, hold the tippet about six or seven inches from the fly in the thumb and forefinger of your stripping hand. Now reach forward with the outside of your pinky and grab a short length of line, bringing the line back inside your hand, palming the line. Now reach forward again and grab another length of line, palming it to the outside of the previous coil. (If you've ever retrieved line with the old hand-twist retrieve, it's exactly the same motion.) Keep doing this, pulling line off the reel as you go, until you have a handful of coils. You can start with a half dozen coils, but with practice you'll be able to do a dozen or even more.

Bring the hand full of line to your casting hand, ensuring that the line from the reel to your hand is tight. You might have to either reel in a bit of line or palm a few more coils to make it tight. Now point the rod tip just slightly above the spot you want to hit and bring the hand with the coiled line back to the side of your head, about equal with your ear. Use the outside of your hand (where your pinky is) to put a bit more tension on the line and just open your hand.

This is how Joe Humphreys coils his line for his special bow-and-arrow cast. The fly and six inches of leader are hanging below his hand.

He then pulls the coiled line back level with his ear.

You'll be amazed to see what looked like a mess of coiled line fire forward and straighten on the water, getting much more distance than you ever would with a traditional bow-and-arrow cast.

Alternatively, if you don't like palming all that line, you can strip the line into bigger coils that hang below your hand. It's not quite as efficient in getting distance because the bigger coils don't pay out quite as well, but if you worry about the line tangling or catching on your body it's a good way of building up confidence. I can tell you from experience that I've never hooked myself using this cast and that it works a lot better than you might think reading the description here, so give it a try on your next small-stream expedition.

Bow-and-arrow casts can be done with a

dry, nymph, or streamer. However, it's best with a single fly, with nothing attached to a leader. A strike indicator or split shot on the leader will take over the cast and make it land awry, and a dry-dropper arrangement of a nymph and dry fly will make the leader tumble and, most likely, tangle. With a dry fly, the tighter the spot the smaller and less air-resistant you want your fly to be. So if a spot calls for a bow-and-arrow cast, remove the size 10 Stimulator on your leader and replace it with something less air-resistant, like a size 16 Adams. It may not be the fly you were hoping to fish, but at least you got it in the right spot, which is the most important task in small-stream fishing.

Releasing the line gives him a long bow-and-arrow cast with a tight loop that fires under low brush.

How to Approach Small Streams

Chapter 7 ....

How to Approach Small Streams

Upstream or Downstream?

One of the most common questions fly fishers new to small-stream fishing ask is, "Should I work upstream or down?" It's an important question because once you begin fishing in one direction or another, you are stuck with that direction unless you haul out of the water and walk overland to a new location. In bigger rivers, where feeding fish might be 50 feet away on the far bank, you can get into a pool, move upstream, then downstream, and then back upstream without disturbing the water if you're careful. The tight quarters in small streams mean that if you work upstream, you will spook all trout once you get close to them, so if you have just fished a quarter mile upstream and turn around and work back downstream, you will be fishing over trout that are spooked and probably not eating. In my experience you might catch a couple of tiny fish doing this, but the decent-sized trout will be hiding and not eating.

The direction you work also depends on what type of fly you will be using. The best way to do this is to work in the direction you are fishing so that you are constantly covering water you have not walked through. If you are fishing in the middle of the day, the water is low, and you see a few caddis flies on the water, you will probably want to fish a dry fly, and dry flies are easier to fish upstream so you should work in that direction. On the other hand, on a slow-moving meadow stream with gentle riffles, you could also work upstream, but perhaps you're in a mood to swing wet flies across and down. By working upstream, you will be casting your flies into a place you just waded through, so a much better idea is to work downstream, so that as you work slowly along

PAGES 156–157: Most small-stream anglers prefer to fish upstream because it is easier to sneak up on the trout—and easier to fish a dry fly.

OPPOSITE: Working upstream with a low profile is the safest bet.

with the current you'll be casting to new water each time, water that has not seen your flies and water you have not yet walked through.

Trout always face into the current, and in the narrow corridors of small streams they are very spooky, living in shallow water and close to the banks their entire lives. Most small-stream anglers prefer to fish upstream because they can approach trout from their supposed "blind spot." You can read all about the physical properties of a trout's eye and calculate the angle of its blind spot, but in practice, out in nature, this knowledge isn't of much use because as a trout feeds it sways back and forth in the current and sometimes darts sideways to eat. So the true blind spot is very narrow. I think the best practice is to assume a trout can always see you, but the fish do seem to be less cognizant of objects behind them. It is still easier to approach a trout from behind, but this may be because the noise and surface disturbance of your wading does not precede you because it is pushed back by the force of the current.

I've proven this empirically many times. I'll see a trout in a stream, feeding happily and undisturbed 30 feet away. Staying directly behind the fish, in its supposed blind spot, without casting to the fish, I've found I can crawl within five feet by moving slowly and carefully, but seldom any closer. If a trout had a true blind spot I should be able to sneak right up to it and touch its tail with my finger, but I can assure you this won't happen. Approaching from upstream, I might not be able to get within 20 feet of the same fish because my entire profile is right in front of it, where a trout sees best and where it is constantly looking.

Sometimes conditions are right for downstream fishing. It's fun to swing a wet fly through small pockets when fishing downstream.

Where Should You Start?

Once you have decided whether to work upstream or downstream, don't immediately jump into the water where you park your car. Water close to access points is more heavily fished, and chances are the fish here are smarter and may have even been spooked by an angler an hour ago. If harvest is permitted in the stream, many of the fish may have graced someone's frying pan last week. If the stream is parallel to a road or trail, take a drive or hike along the banks, and, using the tips you've learned so far about reading the water in small streams, decide which stretch of water is either more productive or more like the kind of water you want to fish. Some small-stream anglers want to try for the biggest fish in the stream and will concentrate on water with a series of deep pools with lots of cover. Others like to catch lots of fish and may prefer the denser population and easier fish found in fast pocket water.

If all the water looks inviting, make it easy on yourself—if you plan to fish downstream, hike upstream a distance so that your walk back to the car will be short. Or if you want to fish both upstream and down, walk upstream and leave a marker along

OPPOSITE: In pocket water like this, fish won't be spooky so you can move quickly.

the banks so you know where you started. Fish upstream a distance, then walk back down to where you began and fish downstream for the rest of the day. It's important to stay well away from the stream when you walk the banks, not only for your own fish but for other anglers you may not have seen. Walking within sight of a small stream is a sure way to spoil the water by spooking fish. In a woodland stream where you are screened from the water by foliage you don't have to stay that far away, but along a meadow stream, where your profile may stand out against the skyline, it's critical that you walk far enough from the stream that you can't see its surface.

How Fast Should You Move?

Regardless of what kind of fly you choose, or whether you work upstream or downstream, the pace you choose is important for success, but it also depends

If most of the trout are this big, it's time to move quickly and fish just the prime spots to avoid handling the tiny, delicate youngsters.

on your goals. If you want to have a relaxing day on the stream, move slowly and carefully no matter what the conditions are. If you want to catch as many fish as possible, you will probably need to speed up. If you only want to catch the biggest fish in a pool, you might want to speed up between pools but slow down once you are in sight of your target pool.

In small streams, trout are not very picky about what fly they take, so a few casts in any given spot is probably enough. The trout you suspect is there will either take your fly on the first good cast or not at all. If it doesn't take it at all, it might be because the fish is spooked, the water might be too cold for it to feed, or in rare cases the fly might be wrong. Repeated casts in the same place are wasted effort. I decided to test this theory on a small brook trout stream near my office one day. I fished my usual size 14 Parachute Adams over a spot that I was pretty sure held a trout or two, and when I didn't get a rise I switched to a large nymph and then a smaller nymph. Finally, I fished a streamer. In the

next pocket, I started with a nymph, and then tried a dry, then a streamer. In every spot except one deep pool where I suspect the fish did not notice my dry fly and I finally got a fish on a nymph fished deep, the trout took whatever fly I threw over them first. In places where I did not get a strike on the first fly I tried, after a half dozen good casts no amount of additional effort produced a fish (and I tried my best to be stealthy so I would not spook them). I've repeated this experiment enough on other streams to have confidence in my statement.

An experienced small-stream angler fishes so quickly and covers so much water that you will be amazed how far you've walked when it's time to head back to the car. I often fish on my lunch hour, leaving what I think is sufficient time to get back to the office, but when I get out of the stream and begin to walk back, I am sometimes shocked at the amount of water I've covered in 45 minutes. The reason for covering so much distance is a combination of not tarrying in the same water for long, and

Experienced small-stream anglers work quickly and cross in the shallow spots.

also pushing ahead and not fishing when the water just ahead of me does not look very productive.

Another reason for moving quickly is that in some small streams most of the trout will be only four or five inches long and each pocket only holds one fish of seven or eight inches. It's probably a good idea to leave the really tiny fish alone because they are more delicate than the larger fish, and a large dry fly in the mouth of a tiny trout can not only damage its jaw beyond healing, but also—if the hook is large enough—penetrate the eye, blinding it. In this case, the best course is to study each pool, determine where the best fish might be, try to catch that fish, and then move on. The best fish in most pools will usually be at the tail of the pool if there is sufficient cover, in the deepest pocket, or adjacent to the largest piece of cover that is in the main flow of current. And if the stream has the aforementioned population makeup—mostly tiny fish with a few larger ones—you should pass up the smaller pockets and just fish the largest pools.

In woodland riffle-and-pool streams, or in meadow streams, where the water alternates between a fast riffle at the head of a pool followed by long glides, your approach should be slow and stealthy. Fish in these pools, as opposed to trout in pocket water where your approach is hidden by the foamy water they lie in, are constantly on the alert, and because the water's surface is smooth and without distortion, fish can spot you from a long way off. Exactly how close you can get to trout in these touchy places varies with the amount of streamside cover, how actively the fish are feeding, and sometimes just the individual personality of each fish. The density of streamside cover relates directly to how close to a trout you can stalk. Against a solid wall of bushes or trees, your profile is broken up. With your profile backlit by the sky, fish will notice every move you make. Fish actively feeding are less wary because they are concentrating on stuff right in front of their noses, and although we don't like to admit it, trout are pretty dumb animals and have

problems multitasking. Sometimes you can get close to one fish in a pool after all the others dart for cover. That one fish might not have spotted you because of its position in the pool, or it might just be bolder than the rest of the fish.

Watch Your Position

Trout have a cone of view on the world above the water's surface. The entire 180 degrees of view possible above the water gets compressed into 90 degrees because of the refractive qualities of water. Tall objects close to a fish are seen best, while objects closer to the horizon get pinched into a narrow band where it is difficult for a fish to distinguish individual objects. This window into the outside world changes with a fish's depth in the water and it gets distorted by riffles, so it's difficult to state how low you should keep your profile to be indistinguishable to a trout. Where fish are spooky I like to stay as low as I can comfortably fish and hope for the best. There aren't many trout in the world worth lying flat on the ground for, so just do your best to stay as low as you can—the lower your profile, the more distorted your silhouette will be.

One of the best ways to keep a low profile in steep pocket water is to fish through a pool, and then stand in the deepest part of that pool to fish the next pool up. Most anglers get out of the pool they've fished and then sneak up the bank to get into position for the next pool, but that presents a higher profile to the fish. By standing in the deep pocket of a pool you can often present just your head level with the next pool up, ensuring that you'll stay in that squished-up band at the bottom of a fish's window—and also mostly in their blind spot. This is an especially good approach when fish lie in the tails of pools and is also the reason I recommend chest waders for all but the tiniest streams.

One of the most threatening movements to a trout is a shadow crossing the water, as it means that something above the surface is moving toward it.

Casting your shadow on a pool is a foolproof way of keeping your nice new dry fly from getting slimed up by a trout. The angle and direction of the sun on bright days will determine how carefully you should approach a pool. Surprisingly, it's actually better to have the sun behind you as long as your shadow does not fall on the water, because trout get blinded when looking directly into the sun—they don't have eyelids so they can't squint. On the other hand, when a trout is between you and the sun it outlines your movements and profile in every detail, so it's wise to move slower and stay lower when illuminated by bright sunlight. Stay in the shade as often as you can, even if it means crossing the brook and getting into a position where you have to cast backhanded. A sloppy approach to a feeding trout is far better than a beautiful cast to one that has bolted for the nearest log in fright.

Current speed will determine how close you can get to a trout in a small stream, and it can be a more important factor than anything else. When you step into a still pool, you'll notice a series of concentric rings spreading out from your feet. Even the most careful approach adds some disturbance to the water, but most anglers don't notice it at all. Trout do. Sometimes the rings don't spook them, and a lot depends on the magnitude of the rings and how actively the fish are feeding. Several trout rising in a pool can actually mask your approach because the rises themselves create rings that compete with yours—as long as you don't spook those feeding fish with your movement above the water.

Assuming you are fishing upstream, faster current makes these rings less distinct. The force of the current retards the upstream progression of your rings, and with enough current speed the ripples made by your wading won't ever get more than a few inches from you. Riffles and rocks mask them as

By using streamside cover and rocks to hide his position and keeping his profile low, Eric Rickstad can work this pool from a short distance away.

well. If you can keep a riffle or a rock between you and a fish, the rings will dissipate before they ever reach a trout's position. Of course, staying out of the water is the best course if you can get away with it, but you have to balance the advantages of staying on the bank with your height above the bank and the amount of room behind you for a cast.

Tailoring Your Approach

Every pool in every stream you fish is as unique as a fingerprint and your approach to each and every piece of water should be gauged first by exploring the water with your eyes from afar. I have a favorite small brown trout stream where the average fish is almost nine inches long, yet most of the fish lie in water no deeper than 18 inches and the deepest pool is probably no more than two feet from top to bottom. There is a lower stretch that flows through a tiny canyon, full of big rocks and pocket water, and although I try to creep along slowly between spots, I can often catch fish from 15 feet away while standing in full view. The rocks and tumbling currents disguise my presence, thus the fishing is fast and easy. Once the stream comes out of the canyon it flows through a wooded meadow, where the current slows, and instead of hiding behind rocks, the fish live in longer glides lined with downed trees on one or both sides of the creek. This water has led to a trout bankruptcy more often than I care to admit. In the easier water down below, I get lulled into a complacent, more relaxed fishing style and I forget to kneel down, creep slowly, and take my time. I have seen brown trout up to 16 inches long in these pools, but I spook them before I even make my first cast on most trips. These fish are usually less than an eighth of a mile from the easier fish and are probably first cousins of the ones I was catching ten minutes before, but they might as well be from another planet.

You can't control how actively the fish feed or their personalities, but you can experiment with how close you can approach fish in each stream you explore. If you see fish rising and they suddenly stop, or if you fish a pool that looks terrific and you don't take any fish, or if you only catch fish in the riffle at the head of the pool, you can safely assume your approach was not careful enough. Your approach should be slow and stealthy (remember trout are more alarmed at quick motions than slow ones), keeping your profile low so that it is hidden against streamside brush or boulders. There is a reason small-stream anglers wear the knees out of their waders quicker than the soles of their shoes. Try to make any false casts short and off to the side of where your final presentation will be so that your line is not in the air above the fish. Then try to make your first cast count, by placing only the fly and tippet over the place you think a trout is feeding.

If you are fishing a stream where most of the trout are tiny and you are trying to sift through them and catch only the bigger fish, make that first cast in the prime location in the pool. On the other hand, if most of the trout are the same size, or if you want to work the water thoroughly and catch as many fish as possible (and it doesn't hurt the ego to catch a bunch of fish some days), then start at the tail of the pool, making two or three careful casts to each likely spot, then moving gradually upstream so you are constantly covering water that has not had a fly line dropped on top of it. Sometimes you'll approach a pool and your first cast will send a fish or two darting to the head of the pool in fright. This may or may not set off a chain reaction, frightening the other fish in the pool. If it's a long, smooth pool with little cover or depth the whole pool might be blown, but in a section with lots of fast, turbulent water or cover, the rest of the fish in the pool might not notice the sentinel warning them.

It's perfectly OK to pass up some pools or pockets just because you don't feel like dealing with difficult conditions. I have a favorite pool on

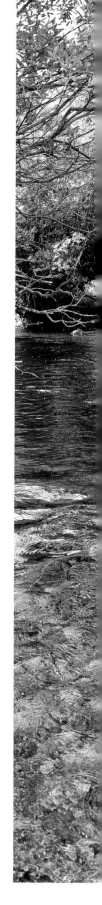

a tiny woodland stream that rushes against a ledge rock wall and forms a pool more than six feet deep in a stream where the average depth is measured in inches. A spring cascades down the rocky bank on the far side, keeping the water cold and comfortable all year long, and the pool's greenish-blue slate bottom and transparent water make it one of the most scenic places I've ever cast a fly. Large trout, at least large for a small mountain stream, regularly leave the depth of the center of the pool for the shallow tail, where they feed on drifting insects. Catching them requires about 20 minutes of careful approach from downstream, almost lying on my belly in cold water, and nine times out of 10 my first cast spooks them. Some days I just don't feel like dealing with these fish. I also know that several fish lie in the head of this pool, under the shelter of the riffle that runs into it, and that I can catch one or two of these guys with just a moderately careful approach as opposed to the major siege needed for the fish in the tail. So, on days when I just don't feel like getting humiliated, I'll cut right into the center of the pool, knowing I'll spook the big fish in the deep water, but that these fish will stay in the depths and not dart up to the head and spook the others.

Some days you might just want to fish dry flies, knowing that you might miss a few trout holed up in the frothy pocket below a waterfall. Maybe you'll encounter a tangle of dead branches hanging over a pool, knowing darned well that you could creep up to them and dangle a nymph down into the brush and probably hook a fish. Or maybe you just don't feel like creeping on all fours to catch that one fish in the tail of a still pool. Don't feel guilty. Go for the easy ones if you like. Small streams are supposed to be places we go for stress relief, to regain egos tramped down by snotty trout in heavily fished rivers.

Fish in the tail of a pool require an extra measure of caution.

 **Chapter 8** ....

Fishing Techniques

Dry-Fly Fishing

▮ WHY DRY?

When most anglers think of small-stream fly fishing they imagine a day of dry-fly fishing. It's easier and more pleasant to cast a dry fly, and the visual appeal of a trout rising to a floating imitation is hard to beat as a pure fly-fishing experience. It's true that the sudden jolt of a fish taking a streamer, the satisfaction of striking to an unseen nymph deep in a pool and feeling the electric beat of a trout pulling against the line, or even the anticipation of a trout tapping at a worm all have their own fascination. But when everything is visual the experience is enhanced further.

A dry fly is also a deadly efficient lure in small streams. Because it is always visible, the angler can track its progress, ensuring that the fly drifts over the perfect spot, and careful observation will show if the fly is dragging unnaturally. It's amazing, even when fishing a nymph with a strike indicator, how far the fly can drift in relation to the indicator and how many strikes can be missed when the leader between the indicator and fly is not tight.

When casting in tight spots, a dry fly can be placed just where you want it, and the fly becomes instantly effective the moment it hits the water. A nymph or streamer has to sink a bit and begin its drift before it is attractive to trout—at least most times. Sometimes a nymph hitting the water appears to be a terrestrial that has just fallen off a branch and fish may pounce on it with no hesitation. Even so, when a nymph hits the water the leader is typically slack and strikes like this may go unseen. With a dry fly there is no doubt that a trout has taken the fly.

PAGES 170–171: Oops. Oh well, you won't land them all.

OPPOSITE: The pleasure of fishing big, bushy dry flies is why many anglers love these tiny waters.

Tight spots like this pool below overhanging branches are perfect for a single dry fly.

It is also easier to fire a bushy, full-hackled dry fly into tight spots. Imagine a log directly in front of you that stretches halfway across the stream, with a tangle of branches hanging off the log that allows only a foot of clearance above the surface. You suspect a trout is lying just on the downstream side of the log, under those branches. A side cast is necessary to get the fly under the branches, but if you try to fish a nymph in this little pocket, the nymph—because it is heavier and less air resistant—flips around at the end of the cast and catches a branch. The momentum of the heavier fly twirls it around a branch like an errant tetherball around a pole and you have no hope of breaking it free. If there is a strike indicator on the leader, the resulting tangle will be even worse. With a dry fly, the delivery is much more predictable and repeatable, and its air resistance slows the fly down at the right moment. Even if it hits the log it will bounce off, its hackles

acting as cushions, dropping the fly to the water right in front of the log.

A dry fly is almost always as effective as any other kind of fly in small streams, unless the water is dirty or in flood, and a dry fly's utility in small streams is in contrast to its sometimes limited use in bigger rivers. Here's why—imagine a trout in a big river, five feet down in a fast run. Even though this fish may be able to see objects on the surface, rising through five feet of water is a struggle against the current. Once the fish rises to the top it gets pushed back by the current, so it has to work to swim upstream, back to its favored location on the bottom. This fish also has access to aquatic larvae drifting in the current throughout the water column, from insects that are hatching or have just been dislodged from the bottom. So instead of fighting through five feet of torrents, it can merely tip up six inches or a foot to feed, where it is protected somewhat by the lower velocity at the bottom of the river, where current speed lessens because of friction with bottom objects. It's only when the amount of food on the surface is so much greater than anywhere else—as when a heavy hatch of mayflies carpets the surface—that this fish begins to feed on floating insects. Trout have an innate ability to balance the benefit of gaining calories from a movement in relation to the calories they obtain by this movement, and they optimize their food intake this way.

Now imagine a trout lying in 15 inches of water in a small stream. Just like the fish in the bigger, deeper river, it can also see every object that drifts above its head. But in this case, it only has to move through slightly more than a foot of water to snatch a floating bug, and in smaller streams, the velocity difference between the bottom and the surface is much less. So to this fish, feeding on a piece of food floating in the surface film takes no more effort than feeding on a nymph floating below the surface. And because nymphs floating at its level are viewed against surrounding rocks and less visible, the fish can spot a floating fly from farther away.

This difference is especially dramatic in the early part of the season. Larger rivers are swollen with runoff, which not only makes food on the surface hard or impossible for the fish to see, but also makes the velocity gradient between the bottom of the river and the surface even more dramatic. In small streams, runoff adds less volume to the stream channel and is often not as dirty as in larger rivers. Colder water temperatures force the trout to be less active, so even if the water in a large river is clear and not raging with runoff, fish are not active enough to forage very far from their positions. In a small stream, the surface might be only inches away and even a trout logy from 45-degree water temperatures might pluck a dry fly from the top.

A trout's appetite for dry flies was hammered home to me one cold April day. It was the beginning of trout season and I snuck away from my office for a quick lunch-hour fix on a small brook close by. The water temperature was 45 degrees and no insects had begun to hatch, so it was not a day I expected to see much action on any kind of fly, but I figured my best luck would be with a nymph fished close to the bottom with an indicator. In the first pool I tried, nothing touched the nymph. In the second tiny pool, a fish rose to my indicator and slowly mouthed it before spitting it out; the water was so cold that the fish rose in a manner I wasn't used to on this small stream, as its tiny brook trout typically splash at the fly with gusto. What a stupid fish, I thought, trying to inhale a pink piece of foam when trailing just below it was a tasty nymph. But when a second fish slapped at the indicator just a few minutes later, I took off the nymph and indicator and replaced them with a single dry fly. It didn't turn out to be the outing of a lifetime, but I was able to catch a few fish on dry flies, probably the earliest in the season I have ever caught Vermont trout on a dry. And I never saw a fish rise, except to my fly, for the entire hour I fished.

Don't reserve a dry fly only for times when you see rising trout or insects in the air. In many of the small streams I fish, I see few rising trout, even at the height of the season when water temperatures are optimum, but catch most of my fish on dries. I'll bet I catch 50 trout on a dry fly fished blind to every trout I catch that I actually see rising. They are quite likely rising all day long, but the irregular nature of the rises combined with the riffled water in most small streams hides most of them from my casual observation.

■ AVOIDING DRAG

Because small-stream trout are seldom picky about the fly pattern they take, and because many of these streams are remote and don't get much fishing pressure, anglers sometimes get sloppy about presentation and don't concentrate as much on avoiding unnatural drag as they do in big rivers with more selective trout. Don't make that mistake. There is a

big difference between a trout scrutinizing a dry fly in a heavily fished river because it's been caught and released numerous times, has abundant food, and can afford to be picky, and a trout that refuses a fly because it does not drift like a natural insect. In their sensitivity to drag, all trout are created equal. Drag is not just something that alerts a trout to something not quite right with a fly; drag is a warning beacon that tells a trout that this thing it is perusing does not behave like every piece of floating food it has seen since birth.

Drag can be as overt as a fly sliding across dissimilar current lanes and leaving a wake behind it or it can be a subtle movement of the fly that is invisible to the angler looking from above. But even the more subtle movements are seen by the trout, silhouetted below against the sky. Trout reactions to a dragging fly are varied. "Short strikes," when fish rise to the fly with a splash but don't connect to the hook, are one clue that drag is a problem. A trout sees a fly that looks tasty and moves toward it with a rush, but as the fish gets closer it sees a bit of drag and closes its mouth rather than inhaling the fly. The trout's momentum pushes it above the surface with its mouth closed, and although the splash looks just like a rise, the fish has not taken the fly. Sometimes a quick strike in this circumstance will hook the fish in the body instead of the mouth. In a small stream, if you get numerous short strikes or foul hook fish in the back or tail, drag—rather than the wrong fly—is usually the culprit.

Controlling drag is more difficult in small streams than in big rivers. In a river, you're presented with longer runs of uniform current, so you can cast a fly and as long as you throw a curve into the cast or throw a little slack in your tippet, your effective drifts are often yards long. In small

Swirling currents like this make a drag-free float difficult. The more uniform currents are easier to fish and usually hold more trout as well.

streams, with shorter pools and shorter stretches of uniform current, drag-free drifts can be only inches long, no matter what you do.

Avoiding drag in a small stream is often as easy as placing the fly a few inches to one side. Trout in small streams, because they don't have a rich food supply, often move two feet to either side of the current lane directly above them to grab a drifting fly. Well-fed fish in larger rivers will seldom move more than a few inches to either side when feeding. Try to pick uniform currents when placing your fly, rather than currents with lots of swirls and eddies that can grab the leader and pull it to one side. If you suspect a trout is lying in churning water just behind a rock, cast to the riffle next to it, where the water moves downstream at a stately pace without conflicting currents. Try all the easy currents first, and if that approach doesn't work, then get tricky and try to manipulate your presentation in the swirling water.

Any time the current closest to you is faster than the place you drop your fly, drag will be a problem. This is especially true in the tails of pools, where water speeds up as it gets constricted by the tail and as it dumps into the riffle below. Here, as soon as it lands, the line just off your rod tip gets snatched downstream under your rod before the line ahead of it can catch up, and the fly drags almost immediately. You can always ignore the fish at the tail of the pool and just try for the ones at the head. The water is just as fast, but there is slower water between your rod tip and the fly, making presentations easier. But in many small streams, the biggest trout prefer the tail of the pool, so eventually you have to develop a way to deal with it.

One way is to keep the rod high after the cast is completed. By keeping the tip of the rod high and

A high rod can help avoid drag over conflicting currents.

Casting on a midstream rock or the bank can help avoid drag just under the tip of the rod.

as much line as possible off the water, you can often keep your line above that faster water at your feet. This works especially well with short casts, and if you can keep all of the fly line in the air and just lay your leader on the water, so much the better. On longer casts, sometimes you can't hold enough line off the water to keep it out of trouble and you have to resort to another trick. The parachute cast helps here because it throws slack into the presentation and gives you a cushion of loose coils that have to pay out before the dragging. You can also overpower your forward cast and aim high so that the line and leader snap forward and jump back against the rod's tension, dropping coils on the water. Or you can underpower the cast and let it drop in a sloppy heap. As long as your fly lands in the right place any of these tricks will work.

Sometimes all it takes to avoid drag is a subtle change in your position, or the position of your rod at the end of the cast. If you are standing just below the tail of a pool, instead of keeping the rod straight out in front of you, sometimes holding it to one side, where the current is slower, will solve the problem. You can also change positions to try to make your line land in a better spot, but in the Lilliputian world of these streams, moving the rod to one side or another can place your line in an entirely different current lane.

Use obstacles in and around the stream to help avoid drag. A rock sticking above the surface is a great place to drop your line since draping the line over a rock keeps the leader beyond it from being pulled downstream. The fly will drag eventually as it drifts downstream of the rock and the

To make a reach cast, immediately begin reaching the rod upstream after the power stroke on the forward cast.

leader then gets yanked upstream, but by that time your fly will have drifted out of the zone where you cast it. Another way to avoid drag, especially in tails of pools, requires more stealth but uses the bank. Instead of fishing the tail of a pool from directly below, in the center of the current, creep off to one side and keep your profile low because as you move to the side you will be more visible to the fish. Cast into the tail of the pool, but from an angle that places most or all of your line on the bank, letting just the leader and a small amount of line land on the water. As with the rock method, the stationary line on the bank keeps the fly from dragging downstream.

The curve or reach cast is a method used often in large rivers to avoid drag. Unfortunately, it's not as useful in small streams because in order to be effective the angler should be opposite or slightly upstream of

a trout. In small streams, with their spooky trout and tight quarters, a reach cast is a luxury available only in the widest pools. But it is sometimes helpful in meadow streams where the angler can creep carefully upstream of a fish and throw a reach cast with enough backcast room. To make this cast, make a standard overhead cast so that the fly lands a few feet above the fish (or its suspected position), but at the last minute—just before the line hits the water—move the rod tip upstream in an exaggerated motion, with your arm extended fully. This puts an upstream hook into the cast, and this loop, because it lies upstream of the fish, will prevent drag until it straightens as it drifts downstream. This cast has the advantage of showing a trout the fly before it sees the leader, but unfortunately in small-stream fishing it makes the angler a lot more conspicuous and more likely to frighten the fish.

Continue reaching upstream and out until your arm is straight.

The result will be a nice curve cast with an upstream hook.

Adding a longer tippet to your leader is another way to take the edge off drag. The leader that you bought from the store was designed to straighten at the end of a proper cast. Adding a longer tippet adds air resistance to the far end of your leader and prevents you from straightening the cast completely, which is just what you want when trying to avoid drag. Most knotless leaders have a level tippet of between 20 and 24 inches seamlessly integrated to the front end of the leader. By adding another two feet of tippet beyond that, you create a leader that straightens well except for the last four or five feet, which gives you decent accuracy but stifles drag, at least for those critical seconds after your fly lands.

Fly choice can also mitigate drag. A fully hackled fly, riding lightly on its tails and hackle tips, does not create as much of a wake as a fly that rides lower in the water because it presents less resistance to the current. Although my favorite small-stream dry fly is a Parachute Hare's Ear, this fly rides low in the water, with its body and parachute hackle pinned to the surface film. In pools where I have frequent drag problems, I often change to a standard Adams dry fly, because it rides higher and seems to make drag less conspicuous.

Another way to address drag with fly choice is to fish with a bigger fly. The bigger the fly, the more force it takes to move it sideways in the current because its mass has some, albeit slight, resistance to movement. On a 4X tippet, a size 12 fly may give you a precious second more of drag-free drift than a size 16, and as the average drift of a fly through a small pool is about five seconds, the difference a larger fly makes is substantial. In fact, I recommend fishing as large a dry fly as you can in small streams. Not only will you get slightly less drag, you'll also be able to spot the fly easily and so

OPPOSITE: In the tail of a pool, the line often loops downstream of the fly, causing difficult drag.

will the fish. I always begin with a size 10 or 12 dry and only switch to a smaller fly if I get frequent splashy rises that don't connect (besides drag, a fly that is too large can also create splashy refusals).

■ WHEN MOVING A DRY FLY IS DESIRABLE

Avoiding drag when dry-fly fishing is critical, but there are times when a slight, subtle, and *controlled* movement of the fly is beneficial. The late Leonard Wright, in his thoughtful book *Fishing the Dry Fly as a Living Insect*, likened drag—as opposed to proper movement of a dry fly—to the difference between an uncontrolled skid by a novice driver on ice and the controlled skid a NASCAR driver uses to slide through a corner.

One method is a simple twitch of the fly. As a fly drifts *drag-free* down the current, a quick lift of the rod tip moves the fly no more than an inch, after which the fly continues to drift drag-free. The fly can be twitched several times during a drift. I stress the words drag-free here, as no amount of fly twitching will turn a presentation with a dragging fly into an effective drift. This presentation works especially well when large aquatic insects, especially stoneflies, are present, whether or not trout are seen rising to them. Chances are the trout have seen a large stonefly twitching across the water in the last day, so that kind of movement may be all it takes to induce them to rise.

Twitching the fly is also warranted during grasshopper season. Most terrestrial insects, when they fall into the water, are completely helpless. Although they may attempt feeble struggles, it's nothing our overt movements with a fly rod can imitate. Grasshoppers, however, have strong kicker legs and often try to oar their way to safety, which only alerts trout to the presence of a hearty meal full of protein. Don't overdo it, though. Many times trout prefer their grasshoppers motionless or with just a subtle, feeble twitch, and while it's a temptation to work a grasshopper fly with a steady retrieve, it more often results in refusals than takes.

Twitching is also effective on windy days with lots of debris on the water, especially in the fall when leaves and twigs and berries rain on the surface. Trout get bombarded by endless junk, and I imagine they sample a lot of it until their taste buds tell them the stuff they've been eating is not adding any calories or helping with their upcoming winter struggle. Then they become reluctant to take any drifting food unless they're sure it's alive. On days like this a twitch reassures them your fly is not just another twig.

During windy days you sometimes have to have nerves of steel or get very lucky. I was fishing a very low, clear woodland stream one breezy October afternoon and tossed my size 14 Yellow Humpy to the head of a favorite pool. I twitched the fly once and what looked like a small trout just dimpled at the fly, so subtle I didn't strike. A foot later, I saw a bigger bulge under the fly but still no connection. I twitched the fly a second time and an 11-inch brown trout, a huge one for this stream, inhaled the fly with a downstream slam. I realized that the same fish had followed the fly down through the pool and made three pokes at it, trying to determine whether it was edible or not, and was finally convinced the fly was alive after the second twitch.

The other technique for moving the fly is called "skating the fly" and is quite different. Skating a fly works best when caddis flies are on the water because it mimics their hatching and egg-laying behavior. Here, you need to be upstream of a fish, so it works better in boulder-strewn pocket water, where you can sneak upstream of a fish and hope the white water and numerous rocks cover your approach. You need a bushy dry fly with lots of hackle, like an Adams or a heavily hackled Elkwing Caddis, and your leader should be greased with fly floatant paste right to the fly so it floats high. Make your cast across the stream, angling slightly downstream, and as soon as the fly hits the water raise your rod tip and sweep the fly across the current, either by moving the rod tip or by stripping line. The idea is to make the fly skate lightly across the top as opposed to digging into the surface, and if the fly throws any spray at all the technique won't work. It works better skating across smooth patches of water as opposed to riffles because the rough surface of a riffle drowns the fly almost immediately. You can also try abruptly dropping your rod tip after skating an inch or two so the fly drifts drag-free. Sometimes trout follow the fly across the current but don't rise, and the appearance of a fly trying to get away and then suddenly giving up is more than they can resist. Trout rising to a skated fly invariably take it with a rush, often clearing the water completely, and sometimes they miss the fly, but it's a fun way to locate trout even if you don't connect to all of them.

■ WHEN YOU FIND RISING FISH

Don't be concerned if you see no rising fish, because as I've said you don't need to see them for great dry-fly fishing. However, when you do it's a rare pleasure and real icing on the cake. Just be aware that they may be tougher than you think. On the rare occasion you see fish in small streams rising to aquatic insects, it's easy to underestimate how snotty they can be.

I used to fish a small mountain stream almost every day in May from noon to 1 p.m. I never saw a fish rise, but always caught 90 percent of my brown and brook trout there on dries. One day I fished it later, around 3 p.m., which is when most aquatic insects in the eastern United States hatch in the early season because water temperatures are at their maximum in mid-afternoon. I was surprised to see size 16 dark, reddish mayflies hatching in good numbers, a rare treat on most infertile mountain streams. Three trout were rising in one tiny pool, and because I was prepared with my usual size 14 Parachute Adams I threw it to the first one. No luck. A half dozen casts produced not a splash to my fly. I tried all three risers, and none of them took the size 14 Adams. Now I know these fish would have taken my attractor fly had there been no hatch, but I had to change to a size 16 Red Quill to take a couple.

I think what happens at these times is that we get lulled into laziness with small-stream fish when there is no hatch, because at those times they aren't picky. The reason they are so agreeable with no hatch on the water is that they are picking at every bug that floats by, and they never see many of the same type. And a lot of their daily diet is terrestrial insects, which can encompass a whole smorgasbord of shapes and sizes. When the rare aquatic insect hatch gets heavy, I don't think the fish refuse a fly because it looks different, they just ignore it because

they have the image of a size 16 fly with a red body and gray wings in their search pattern. I don't think they ever really *see* other flies.

If you do see a hatch in a small stream and the trout respond to it, resist the urge to fish that favorite attractor pattern and put on something close to what they are eating. Small-stream fish are not as selective as Bighorn River brown trout and don't need an exact imitation of the natural, but you'd better be close. And, as always, these fish will be ultra-sensitive to drag so do everything you can to reduce it and don't get sloppy.

For a trout, the best place to take advantage of a hatch is in the tail of a pool where the water is smooth and all the currents converge. In a big river, they can't and won't all swim down to the tail

When you encounter a hatch and rising trout on a small stream, replace the bushy attractor fly with a more precise imitation of what is hatching.

because it's too much effort and too much of a risk. But in small streams, the tail of the pool is often just the flip of a tail away, so you will find most of the fish concentrated there, which only makes the fishing more difficult. Trout are not easy to approach in the smooth current that shows the outside world well, and drag is more pronounced where the water quickens before it drops off into the next riffle. Keep your profile low, try to approach the fish either from the bank or from the pool below, and throw lots of slack with a parachute cast.

Nymph Fishing

On those rare days when trout are reluctant to come to a dry fly in small streams, nymphs can save the day. If you have experience nymph fishing with indicators on bigger rivers, you'll find that nymph fishing in small streams is not quite the same game. Drifts are shorter and shallower, and where in a large river you may have six feet of drift above a fish's suspected location in order to place your fly in just the right spot, in small streams you may have only a foot or so of drift before your fly is out of the game.

In most rivers, the strategy is to cast well above a spot with a pair of nymphs, one tied to the tippet, and the second tied to another piece of tippet material that is tied to the bend of the first hook with a clinch knot. Often a split shot of soft weight is added to the leader a few feet above the flies and a strike indicator is used both to detect strikes and to watch and control the drift of your flies. In rivers, the dilemma is to get your flies close to the bottom and away from the faster current at the surface, at the same time keeping the flies from moving faster than the surface currents and acting unnaturally. In small streams, this kind of rig is a formula for big trouble. Placement of your nymph in small streams, because of streamside brush and short drifts, is critical and it is tough to be precise with all that stuff hanging off your leader. Also, getting your fly too close to the bottom puts it in a place where it is difficult for trout

to see it, as they can see drifting food above them much easier than food sliding down at their level. Not to mention the frequent hang-ups on the bottom, which result in either a lost fly or a disturbed pool when you have to wade in to retrieve the fly.

▪ NAKED NYMPHING

The cleanest and most precise way to fish nymphs in a small stream is with a single fly on the leader. No indicator, no split shot, no dropper. This naked nymph fishing is the way it was practiced for almost 100 years, before we leaned on the strike indicator crutch, and it's a real pleasure to be in a situation where it's effective. It can be done with a short line and a high rod, for fish that are 10 feet away or less, or at more than 10 feet away with a lower rod tip.

For short-line casts, it's best to cast straight upstream just above a likely pocket. Your rod tip should stop at about the 10 o'clock position in front of you and the rod tip should then be brought back toward you and a little off to one side as the fly drifts downstream. Stripping line to gather it is not recommended—because of the very short line you are fishing, gathering line will pull the fly downstream and make it drift unnaturally. If you can, try to keep just the leader or even a part of the leader on the water and all the fly line above the surface, suspended from your rod tip. You'll notice that the line below the rod tip forms a slight curve with the concave surface facing you. This little belly is your strike indicator. If at any time that belly twitches or begins to straighten, set the hook with a quick but short twitch of the rod tip. At this distance you need little effort to sink the hook in a trout's jaw.

If the light is such that you can see your leader floating on the surface, you can also watch the leader for little jumps or hesitations. You may also try scoring the middle of your leader slightly with the edge of your thumbnail, just enough to put a small pigtail in it. Any time the pigtail straightens, set the hook. Sometimes you may see trout dart or flash at your fly as well, and this method lets you watch your leader and the fly at the same time because they are close enough that you can see both the pigtail and the location of your fly with the same intent gaze.

When casts get beyond 10 feet it's tough to keep all the fly line off the water. In this case, keep your rod tip at the normal level, closer to the water, and strip line to gather slack as the fly drifts back to you. For these longer presentations, watch the junction of your leader and fly line or put a pigtail in your leader. And, yes, if you must resort to a strike indicator, which are sometimes useful in deep pools and on longer casts, make it a small one, the smallest you can find. You'll seldom have weight on your leader you need to suspend with a big indicator, and bigger indicators are likely to spook trout in the shallow water of small streams. A small piece of yarn, secured to the leader with a slip knot and dressed with dry-fly paste, won't hinder your cast much and is subtle enough that it won't land with a splash and spook wary trout.

DRY DROPPERS

My other problem with using strike indicators in small streams is that often fish eat them, and once a fish comes to an indicator and the instinctive hook set that follows, it will be spooked and you'll be left with a trout that won't feed for awhile. You can solve that problem, and the decision whether to fish a nymph or a dry, with a dry dropper arrangement. Rigging a dry dropper is simple. You tie a high-floating dry fly like a Stimulator or grasshopper pattern to the tippet as normal, then tie a piece of tippet

Meadow streams are good places to try a hopper/dropper combination—just watch your casts on the tall grass along the edge.

material, the same diameter as your dry-fly tippet, to the bend of the dry-fly hook. Then just tie a nymph onto this tippet.

This method works better in more open streams because the dry dropper rig does not cast as well as just a single fly, and it's tough to place the flies into a tight spot because two flies on the leader opens up your casting loop and hinders your ability to throw a tight loop under low branches. Two flies catching in high grass on your backcast in a meadow stream, or in trees just over your head in a woodland stream, are twice as hard to untangle because the centrifugal force of the second fly whipping around the first fly that gets tangled exponentially increases the amount of time you'll spend unwinding the chaos.

Most advice on nymph fishing tells you to make the length of the dropper to which you attach

the nymph about one-and-a-half times the depth of the water, because the nymph seldom hangs directly below the dry, but at more of a 45-degree angle. In small streams, I prefer to make my droppers shorter. It is not as hard to sink a nymph in a small stream as it is on a large river because the velocity gradient from top to bottom is not as sharp, so your nymph will sink faster anyway. Trout in small streams are more likely to feed on a nymph that is just below the surface. Besides, the longer the dropper between the nymph and the dry, the more difficult casting becomes, so with a dropper between four and eight inches long, casting is smoother, tighter, and more accurate.

Because your dry fly is both a lure in itself and an indicator, it must float well and be highly visible. Flies with buoyant hair like the Stimulator and Elk Hair Caddis or heavily hackled flies like the Royal and Ausable Wulff work better than more delicate parachute flies or low-floating terrestrial imitations. Keep the dry fly dressed with desiccant powder every five minutes, and if the dry sinks frequently try an unweighted nymph or soft-hackle wet fly as the dropper. Fish are often attracted to the big dry because they see it first, and end up taking the nymph just below the surface because it is an easier meal.

Nymphs can also be fished swung in the current, which I'll describe in the next section on wet-fly fishing, because the line between nymphs and wet flies is a slim one anyway.

Wet-Fly Fishing

While the dry fly is the most common and effective type of fly for most tumbling mountain streams and fast-moving woodland creeks, a soft-hackle wet fly, swung in the current, is the favorite technique of many small-stream experts who frequent low-gradient

In a low-gradient woodland stream, sometimes swinging a wet fly downstream is the best approach.

Swinging a wet fly downstream is a relaxing way to cover a lot of water.

streams found especially in the Midwest. In these smoother waters where trout are more aware of surface disturbance, swinging a wet fly presents the fly to the fish before they see the leader or line.

Although wet flies and nymphs can be fished dead drift downstream—imitating drifting insects—by casting lots of slack or feeding line, the most common way is to swing them across the current. A fly sliding sideways in the current probably imitates swimming mayfly nymphs or caddis pupae, and some adult insects swim underwater to lay their eggs. It's quite likely that a swung wet fly also imitates a tiny baitfish. I have seen miniature sculpins, after they hatch in late spring, that are no longer than a size 12 wet fly hook and I have no doubt that trout relish these smaller, eas-

ier-to-catch sculpins as much as they like the larger three-inch adults.

Getting a swing across the current in a small stream presents special problems because the cast must be made at some angle to the current rather than straight upstream or downstream, perhaps one reason many prefer upstream dry-fly and nymph fishing in tiny waters. As soon as you try to cast across the stream you will most likely face some kind of backcast obstructions, so a roll cast or a snap-T cast is almost mandatory unless you are fishing an open meadow. False casts shouldn't even be considered—not only do they increase the chances of getting snagged, they also flick water from your fly, which you don't want, because a wet fly should sink as soon as it hits the water and a damp fly sinks better than one that's been dried off. This is a wonderfully low-energy, relaxing way of fishing. You work downstream with the current, make a simple roll cast, let the fly swing, and then just flick the fly back to the water. When working downstream with a wet fly in creeks with mud or silt bottoms, try to stay out of the water or as close to the bank as you can. A plume of muddy water that follows you downstream is a sure way to turn off any trout that might be feeding.

In meadow and woodland streams with a strong central thread of current and slow water to either or both sides of it, the best way to fish a wet fly or swung nymph is to cast the fly into the fast water and let it swing into the slower water as it drifts. This way you drop your fly into a place where the splash won't spook trout, and it sinks and then swings into the slower water along the edge of the fast, which is where you will find most trout. Again, because of the conflicting currents found in most small streams, the rod tip should be held high enough to keep most of the fly line off the water; otherwise, the currents closest to you will suck the fly line under and limit your ability to control the fly's swing and to detect a strike. If you are fishing from the bank, this is even more critical to keep the line from hanging up on the grass or debris in front of you.

Once the fly has completed its swing and is hanging directly below your rod tip, the action might not be over. Usually trout see the fly on the swing, and you can increase the coverage of your swing by moving the rod tip off to one side so that the fly continues its swing into different water. A wet fly can also be just as effective on the retrieve. There are many ways to retrieve a wet fly—long, slow, steady pulls; quick, short darts; or a hand-twist retrieve, which seems to produce an action that ordinary strips through your fingers can't duplicate. The hand-twist retrieve, if you are not familiar with it, is done by rotating your hand around the line, alternating the inside of your thumb and the outside of your pinky, palming the line after each rotation. Try all types of retrieves until you find the one most attractive to the fish—it varies between streams

and even from one day to the next for reasons unknown to anything without fins.

Pocket water, with its restless, alternating currents that never settle down long enough for a decent wet-fly swing, presents a special set of challenges. No sooner does the fly land than the current sweeps it from fast water to almost motionless pockets, and then on to the next swirling pocket. A fly that switches speed and direction like this seems to raise a warning flag to trout. Here you need to regain control of your fly from the current and lead it through the churning water at a constant rate. This calls for a high rod to keep most of the line off the water, and when the fly swings through uniform current let the water do the work. If it slides into a spot of clear water behind a rock, lead the fly through the pocket with the rod tip until it slides into more current, and continue on through the pockets until the fly is hanging directly below you. I've also found that twitching the fly with tiny pulses of the rod tip can add to its attractiveness in pocket water.

Streamer Fishing

Although not the first choice of most small-stream fly fishers, streamer fishing can sometimes provoke a strike when nothing else works, particularly in high, dirty water, or in deep, frothy plunge pools where trout may have trouble spotting a drifting dry fly or nymph. Streamers are also effective for weeding out the one big brown trout in a half mile of water without bothering all the little brook trout if you're after a monster.

In featureless slow water, such as you might find in boggy, lowland streams, streamers may be the best bet if no fish are seen rising. It's difficult to fish nymphs in slow, deep water with no visible obstructions to pinpoint the location of trout, but you can cover a lot of water with a streamer because you can strip it through 20 or 30 feet of water as opposed to the short drift you might obtain with a nymph or wet fly. Plus, trout will move a lot farther for a streamer than a nymph, if—and this is a big if—trout are in the mood to take one.

Besides a rise of water, in small meadow streams I've often had spectacular luck with streamers when cows get into the stream and temporarily muddy the water. I remember one morning when I was fishing upstream of my house in the middle of the summer. I had fished up through a half mile of water with a dry fly and a nymph without taking a single fish. Suddenly, in the middle of that bright, clear morning the water turned as muddy as it would in a sudden rainstorm. I grumbled to myself that the cows in the meadow just upstream had ruined my chance to catch a fish that morning, but as I turned around to walk home, I thought better of the idea and put on a small sculpin. Fishing it upstream through a riffle I had just covered carefully with a nymph without even a single strike, I took a half dozen rainbows and browns on the tiny streamer until the water cleared. Just as quickly the trout switched off and then I finally walked home.

A small streamer is often effective fished just as a wet fly, swung on a tight line in the current without any motion added by the angler. This makes sense especially when you consider that trout may be taking your wet flies for a tiny baitfish anyway. Try it first before any other because it disturbs the water less than a fly with added motion.

The most productive part of a streamer fishing drift may not be in the drift at all but in the retrieve, so retrieve the fly almost to your rod tip before making another cast. Unlike a retrieve with an insect imitation like a nymph, which is not very credible because few insects dart upstream against the current (if insects swim at all, it is usually downstream or across currents), a baitfish darting upstream is a natural behavior. Just gauge your retrieve to what you are trying to imitate. Small baitfish don't make foot-long bursts upstream when they swim, so don't expect many trout

if you retrieve a size 12 streamer as fast as you would a big Woolly Bugger in a large river. You can also add lifelike twitches to a streamer as it swings across the current. Either short strips or a slight pumping of your rod tip will make the fly look like a minnow or crayfish that is struggling against the current, trying to swim upstream but not making much progress. Stripping the fly is especially productive in high or dirty water because it differentiates the fly from sticks and other non-edible debris floating downstream.

Streamers are also deadly fished upstream. Sometimes, like at the foam at the base of a waterfall, it's the only way to make an effective presentation. Or, if you've been working upstream with a

A deep pool like this might be a good place to try a streamer.

dry fly but not getting many strikes, it doesn't make sense to cast back over water you've already waded through. It's often said that trout are afraid of a baitfish that swims directly at them because prey doesn't slam right into predators, which is true, so in fishing a streamer downstream cast to one side of where you suspect a trout may be hiding and bring your streamer back through that slot. Baitfish that are crippled or frightened, especially sculpins, try to escape downstream because they know they won't make any headway trying to fight the current.

Streamers can be fished dead drift, which imitates a baitfish drifting downstream and gets the fly deeper. Fish a streamer dead drift just as you would a nymph, watching your line or leader for the slightest twitch. Trout take streamers with more gusto than they do nymphs because they are attacking their prey rather than inhaling it, so there is seldom any doubt when a trout takes a streamer, even when dead drifting without a strike indicator. You can also add motion to your streamer. Remember, though, that whatever motion you add is in addition to whatever push the current is already giving to the fly. The best advice I can give is to strip line until you see it go tight, then stop and let the fly drift for a second, then begin another strip. Trout usually take the fly during the pause and you'll either see the line jump forward as they do, or you'll feel them as you begin the next strip.

Wild Trout, Hatchery Trout, and Differences Between the Species

It is relatively easy to tell the difference between recently stocked hatchery fish and wild fish (a trout that was born in a stream via natural reproduction). The first clue that a stream is hatchery supported is when all of the fish are very close in size. Hatcheries typically stock fish from the same generation, and since their diet and environment are very uniform, the fish will be within an inch or so in size between individuals. The second clue is the coloration of the fish. Although hatchery fish can be made more colorful by adding certain foods to their diet, most are fed a commercial fish pellet that produces trout with an overall dull, gray tone with few bright colors. The third clue is the condition of the fins on the fish. Hatchery fish are raised in crowded conditions, sometimes over a rough concrete bottom, and between fish fighting each other for space and rubbing against hatchery tanks, the fins become rough along their trailing edges. A sure giveaway is a clipped adipose fin. This is a small, smooth fin between the big dorsal fin and the tail of a trout, and hatcheries sometimes clip this fin so that fish raised under man-made conditions can be easily identified throughout their lives.

Wild trout have smooth, clean fins, brighter colors, and vary in size. In a wild population, you will catch the occasional tiny fish under six inches long and, if lucky, a large fish well beyond the norm. Wild fish usually fight better when hooked than hatchery fish, and most anglers believe they taste better. Wild fish are more difficult to catch because they have learned to recognize, from birth, the foods in a stream that are safe to eat. When hatchery fish are first stocked and don't get fish pellets fed to them every day, they sample all manner of edible and inedible drifting food until they become acclimated to a stream diet—although if they survive long enough they can get as picky about what they eat as wild fish.

Most trout caught in small streams will be wild because fishery managers don't stock trout in streams where fishing pressure is light and few fish will be returned to the public. It's expensive to raise trout to catchable size, and if a stream has little or no fishing pressure, it doesn't make sense to pour the taxpayers' revenue down the drain. You'll be more likely to find hatchery trout in small streams in the South because summer water temperatures in warmer climates often reach the lethal limit for trout. In order for anglers there to have any trout fishing at all, fish need to be stocked every year because few survive long enough to spawn.

Although all trout, even those from hatcheries, have some degree of built-in wariness, hatchery fish are less likely to bolt for cover when a shadow crosses a pool or they see a hand waving in the air because they have been conditioned to the presence of humans. Hatchery fish also do not seem to have the same innate sense of hydraulics as wild trout, and they may spend more of their time in the middle of a fast current or in the stagnant water at the edges of deeper pools, where wild trout are more often found in the halfway water—current fast enough to bring them food but not so fast they exhaust themselves holding a position. Hatchery fish have actually been observed wasting away in current that makes them work harder than the return in calories they receive by feeding there.

Among the various species of wild trout, there are characteristics of each species that make finding and catching them easier (or at least giving you an excuse when you don't catch any). Bear in mind, though, that fish do have individual personalities and that the conditions in one stream can make them behave differently from those in another, and that even daily changes can change the feeding and movements of trout.

Brook trout evolved in cold, infertile waters and, as a result, they sample every piece of drifting food that looks remotely edible. Anglers say they are more gullible or less smart than other trout species, but it's more a matter of their adaptation to a less fertile environment. Regardless of whether you call them stupid or well-adapted, fly selection for brook trout is not as critical as with other species. They take dry flies and submerged flies with equal gusto, and will rise to a dry fly in water temperatures that keep other trout glued to the bottom. Brook trout like to hide relatively close to cover and will most likely be found near larger rocks and logs.

Rainbow trout are able to feed in faster current than other species, and will often be found suspended in mid-water, even in relatively fast current. They are just as likely to use the broken surface of a riffle or deep water when danger threatens, so they are often found in more open areas in a stream. Rainbows can get more selective than brook trout or cutthroats and often feed on tiny insects throughout the day, so if success is lacking on a stream with rainbows it's a wise idea to try a size 20 or smaller fly.

Brown trout evolved in richer environments than any other trout and are inclined to feed in spurts, especially when food is abundant. Brown trout streams can seem lifeless when the fish aren't interested in feeding, but in a matter of hours the fish can get ravenous and much easier to catch. Brown trout are more likely than any other species to eat baitfish and crayfish, so a larger nymph or a streamer will often draw strikes when smaller flies don't. Brown trout are especially covetous of overhead cover and will be found most often near logs and under streamside vegetation. They usually are found in slower, deeper water than rainbows.

Cutthroats, like brook trout, evolved in more sterile environments, so they have a reputation of being easy to fool. They are more often found in slow water than fast, and when food is abundant they are inclined to move into very shallow gravel bars and the edges of a stream. These are spots that are often overlooked by small-stream anglers, so when in cutthroat country, pay as careful attention to the shallow spots as the deeper pockets.

Small Stream Care and Ethics

 **Chapter 9** ....

Small Stream Care and Ethics

With the exception of southern and desert tailwaters that emerge full-blown from the base of a dam, keeping water cold enough for trout in regions where groundwater is too warm to support them, all major trout rivers depend on small streams for their existence. Small streams are the veins that feed cold, pure water into rivers. They collect organic matter that falls into them and grind it into food for small invertebrates that support the running-water food chain. And in many cases, small streams offer the cold, clean water and gravel beds required for trout spawning where bigger rivers, lower down in a valley, are too silted and warm for successful spawning and rearing of young trout.

Thus small streams offer much more than just a place for you to enjoy fly fishing. Because fishing pressure is light to nonexistent on many small streams, environmental insults are often ignored because no one notices them or cares. You will seldom see patently obvious problems in small streams.

It's not likely that you'll come upon a large rusty pipe leaching toxic waste into a tiny woodland stream. Most of the problems you see will be the result of sloppy or questionable land-use practices that the average hiker might not even notice as a problem. Logging roads built too close to small streams, road construction without adequate silt traps, culverts that are too high to allow passage of fish, brush removal right down to the riparian zone, or livestock allowed to graze right down to the waterline are the kinds of issues to watch.

As a small-stream angler, it is incumbent upon you to safeguard these precious resources. On my

PAGES 196–197: Small streams are the lifeblood of bigger rivers, and issues such as strips of riparian cover between agricultural fields and streams are essential to keep water clean and cold.

OPPOSITE: This stream has a healthy riparian zone. It will stay cooler during the summer, survive floods better, and will provide more food for its trout.

This tiny stream holds trout, but is severly overgrazed in the foreground and channelized in the background. Its potential for producing trout and providing cool water to the bigger river it flows into is compromised.

way to work every day, I pass a tiny tributary to the Battenkill that emerges from alkaline springs on the side of a low mountain. Within a half mile, the brook is dammed near the large entrance to an estate that contains a famous art gallery. It's a pretty little pond framed by the back side of the mountain and a large hay field. I'm sure thousands of people have enjoyed the view over the years. Less than a quarter mile downstream from the outflow of the first dam is a second pond, located in the front yard of a cute little colonial house. I'm sure the owners of the house love their pond. And just downstream of this second pond lays a third, much larger than the other two, hidden in the woods beside a huge estate not visible from the road.

All of these ponds were built long ago, before the resource managers recognized the value of small tributaries to large rivers, and it would probably be impossible to get them removed without high legal costs and bad PR that neither the state fish and game department nor the local Trout Unlimited chapter can afford. Yet these tiny, scenic, seemingly innocuous ponds block trout from running up the tributary to spawn and their shallow basins warm the water beyond the tolerance level for trout on hot summer days. So not only is this tiny brook lost to small-stream anglers, its cold water inflow and spawning potential is lost to the larger river a few miles downstream. Over the years the Battenkill has adjusted to the loss of its input, but as more and more of its veins are blocked by the plaque of numerous small ponds, its fishery suffers.

It's much easier to stop small-stream problems before they occur than to remove old, grand-

This small pond looks pretty, but it warms and stagnates a small trout stream and the dam at its base keeps trout from the spawning grounds in its upper reaches.

fathered diversions. What can you do? Your first step should be to get a photo of the issue. Nothing presents the problem better than a visual smoking gun. Your next step should be to contact your local Trout Unlimited chapter, Federation of Fly Fishers club, or local land trust. One person alone whining about a problem on a small stream is a crackpot. Five people is a bunch of crackpots. One hundred people is a political force. If the problem is on private land, tread lightly. The worst thing you can do is drive up to the house of a hard-working dairy farmer, red in the face, and scream about his cattle in the river. Believe it or not, getting money to fix problems on small streams is seldom the issue, nor is getting the proper permits if you can find the right person in the state or local government. The biggest issue is getting landowner permission. The

best approach is to find someone in the local Trout Unlimited chapter who knows the farmer. The problem can be brought up in conversation over coffee, with a rationale for fixing the issue, a solution that benefits both the stream and the farmer, and an offer to pay for fencing and its maintenance for years to come. Keeping cattle off an eroded bank stabilizes the riparian zone and the farmer ends up with a net gain in grazing land.

Issues on public land pose no problem with landowner permission, and forest service and Bureau of Land Management (BLM) managers are required to protect resources for all users, at least theoretically. Their problems are usually manpower to inspect logging roads or road-building projects, as well as the money and political will to fix them. Local fishing clubs can offer demonstrated public support, manpower, and money to help the strained resources of government resource managers and once these elements are in place the combined synergy of grass-roots support and government can be extremely powerful. Most government resource managers have public relations goals to fulfill, and in my home state U.S. Forest Service personnel have even been involved in habitat restoration projects on private land, outside of the National Forest boundaries. It's great community public relations for them and earns them points with their bosses. Luckily, small-stream habitat projects by nature require small amounts of money and manpower unless they are massive eroded zones near roads or heavily grazed land.

Safeguard Your Stream

Here are some of the issues to look for as you are fishing:

■ Bridge or road construction without hay bales to filter silt that results from construction.

■ Culverts that are built too high to allow fish passage at low water.

■ Livestock grazing or plowing right down to the banks of a stream. Unstable stream banks pour silt and gravel into streams, forming a wide, shallow channel that warms the water in summer and destroys fish habitat.

■ Logging or landowner clearing close to the banks of a stream. Regulations vary by state and region from no required buffer zone to as much as 50 feet. Even if no buffer zone is required by law, often resource managers, especially fish biologists, can intervene and make suggestions that will protect stream banks.

■ Unimpeded runoff from mines, parking lots, or any other man-made areas that can concentrate toxic chemicals.

■ Channel straightening after major floods. This is one scenario that requires immediate action, as one bulldozer in a small stream can destroy habitat for generations. It's tough to stop this kind of project when life or property has been lost in a recent flood, but all channelization does is destroy habitat and increase stream velocity farther downstream. Natural meanders in a stream decrease flood water velocity and also force water underground at the outside of each bend, keeping water temperatures cool during hot summer months.

Heavy equipment in a river is always a cause for alarm.

Thus far I've discussed stewardship of the habitat, which I believe is the key to preserving small-stream fishing for the next generation. What about catch-and-release fishing? Isn't that the future for our small-stream fisheries?

It is nearly impossible to remove enough fish by angling to ruin a trout fishery. There will always be trout that live in spots impossible to fish, and these remaining fish will spawn and restock a stream, if the habitat will support them. It takes only a few pairs of spawning fish to restock miles of river in just a few years. Catch-and-release fishing is a sociological tool for stockpiling more and bigger fish for the current generation. It makes your fishing more productive, but it won't do a thing for your children's fishing if the habitat is destroyed. If you have the time and energy to work for reduced limits and better regulations on small streams *and* to fight for the maintenance and improvement of habitat, more power to you. But most of us have busy lives and limited resources, and putting your energy into habitat work is a far more admirable allocation of your time.

You can establish habits that will protect and improve short-term fishing every time you venture into a small stream. Keeping no fish, or just a few small ones, will make the experience better for everyone who enjoys the resource. Small-stream trout are fragile; barbless hooks ensure that you release fish with no damage to their anatomy. In fall or spring, if you see fish spawning in shallow gravel, get out of the river and be very careful not to step on their redds or gravel nests. When you wade a small stream, try to disturb as little of the water as possible so that the next person fishing can enjoy fish that are not spooked and off the feed.

We've learned how wading gear, especially felt-soled wading shoes, carries invasive organisms from one watershed to the next. Felt offers tiny nooks and crannies that host spores of invasive organisms like whirling disease (a parasite that is lethal to small trout) and didymo (an invasive algae that can choke a streambed), as well as organisms we may not even have identified as a problem yet. Felt takes days to dry,

Small-stream trout survival increases if you use barbless hooks, handle the fish quickly and gently, and keep them in the water or only remove them briefly.

and by staying wet it helps spores stay alive, where they can be transferred to another watershed. Wear rubber-soled wading shoes with metal studs (without studs they are not as safe as felt soles on slippery rocks) and clean, inspect, and dry all mud and other debris from all of your wading gear before entering a different watershed. If you always fish the same stream these safeguards are unnecessary, but today's fly fishers can travel around the world in a matter of hours and you could introduce a new and destructive organism into a pristine stream just by walking in it.

Small pockets of erosion in a small stream can be kept from growing by stabilizing the bank with shrubs and small trees. In the spring before leaves appear, cut willow or red osier dogwood shoots (or whatever shrub is common along the stream) and stick them into soft mud or sand just above the high-water line. Their roots will help stabilize the bank, and at high water their stems will collect silt and debris that will eventually build up a new and more stable stream bank. Coming back to places where you've done your small part to reduce erosion, and seeing the new stable bank full of vegetation is one of the most satisfying moments you can have on a trout stream.

Acknowledgments

Although I've fished in small streams over the past 40-plus years from Maine to California, and from Alaska to Chile, it's impossible to get a sense of what all the small-stream regions in the United States alone are like, much less those throughout the world. In the process of writing this book, I communicated with small-stream anglers across North America. You'll be happy to know (and I sure was) that small-stream trout seem to behave the same no matter where they're located, so you can be confident that the tactics and flies I suggest here will work in your streams.

Thanks to the following people for giving me an idea of what their small-stream conditions are like throughout the season, and thanks for reassuring me that despite regional differences in geology and trout species, the fish all respond eagerly to the same casts, flies, and approaches: Jim Babb, Buzz Cox, Kirk Deeter, Scott Farfone, Russ Ford, Larry Gavin, Josh Greenburg, Joe Humphreys, Ted Leeson, John Muir, Tim Romano, John Shewey, Doc Thompson, Nick Volk, Bob White, and Derek Young.

I'd also like to express my appreciation to the fine small-stream anglers who let me follow them around with my camera while shooting images to help illustrate this book: Jeremy Benn, David Carmona, Buzz Cox, Marshall Cutchin, John d'Arbeloff, Kirk Deeter, Scott Farfone, Joe Humphreys, Scott McEnaney, John Muir, Christopher Nevitt, Jason Newell, William Quick, Eric Rickstad, Wayne Rock, Tim Romano, Barry Unwin, Mary Vogelsong, Rick Wagner, and Rick Wollum. And thanks to Sony for making such wonderful cameras and lenses.

James Daley is a wizard with computer graphics and worked patiently with me to create the groundwater map and the wonderful fish illustrations that decorate the map.

Special thanks to Joe Humphreys, who at 83 is still hard to keep up with on small brook trout streams. He generously showed me some of his special techniques developed over eight decades of trout fishing, allowed me to be the first one to detail his special bow-and-arrow cast in print, and even bought me lunch!

Special thanks to Robin Kadet for taking photos of the parachute cast and reach cast on our backyard river, for letting me spend so much time on small streams across the country, and for being the most incredible human being I have ever known.

Index